You are FORGIVEN

EMBRACING GOD'S
FORGIVENESS IN OUR LIVES

*Angela Perritt, Jen Thorn, Joy Forney,
Whitney Daugherty and Joan Shaffer*

LOVE GOD GREATLY MINISTRY

ISBN-13: 978-0692759714 (Love God Greatly)

ISBN-10: 0692759719

Library of Congress Cataloging-in-Publication Data

Printed in the United States of America

21 20 19 18 17 16
6   5   4   3   2   1

Sweet friend, embrace God's love,
hold fast to His grace and be forever changed
by His amazing gift of forgiveness.

You are loved.

You are forgiven.

Contents

Foreword

The steadfast love of the Lord never ceases,

his mercies never come to an end,

they are new every morning,

great is your faithfulness.

Lamentations 3:22-23

"MAMA, DO YOU STILL love me when I make such stupid mistakes?" My sweet teenager, many years ago, was curled up on the couch in an almost fetal position, deeply regretting something she had done and was condemning herself over and over again for not refraining from the foolish behavior.

"I love you if you had made 10,000 mistakes. I love you because you are mine. I love you even in spite of the mistakes you will make the rest of your life. You are so precious to me that I can hardly refrain from kissing your sweet head a million times right now."

A tiny smile curled on her lips. I stroked her hair and told her that God's love became more precious to me each day, because the older I got, the more I sinned, even when I wish I could be good. And this truth made me love Him for His gracious love given freely every single day.

The truth is, all of us know that deep inside we are broken. We want to be good, to practice patience, to be generous of heart, yet our petty selves accuse us of countless ways we fail to live up to our own standards on a daily basis. And we know we fall short in a thousand ways of God's ways for us. But now that I am 63, I have learned that His love for me is beyond measure, and His forgiveness already extends to every day of my life. His mercy is never ending. This truth has changed my life.

Just this morning, I was awakened by a sunrise outside the bedroom window. Pink and coral shadows danced on the clouds and seemed to say, "This day is holy, a day to celebrate, because I am here. My love and mercy are the starting points of your day. Remember me and live in my joy."

And then I remembered one of my favorite verses that speaks to me every time I see a beautiful sunrise. The steadfast love of the Lord *never* ceases, His mercies never come to an end, *they are new every morning.* Every single morning when we awaken, God's mercy sees our frailty and provides for a covering of grace through every moment we fall short of perfection. Every day, we can live in the freedom of knowing that we are forgiven.

This profound truth is so vitally important to being able to love God fully, and to live in the deep joy and freedom He wants us to experience every day.

The truths of His forgiveness written in this book will transform your life every day. His life exchanged for your life means you will never have to feel separated from Him again, but every day you can curl up in His abiding love, walk in His gracious mercy, and breathe free from the burden of guilt. Our heavenly Father waits to show you His goodness because it is at the very core of His heart.

It is my hope and prayer that everyone who studies these profound truths will understand and experience His complete forgiveness of every sin you will ever commit, every flaw, every imperfection... and that you will live in the peace His Spirit brings to carry us through every day until we see Him face to face.

Sally Clarkson. July. 2016

Welcome

WE ARE GLAD you have decided to join us in this Bible study! First of all, please know that you have been prayed for! It is not a coincidence you are participating in this study.

Our prayer for you is simple: that you will grow closer to our Lord as you dig into His Word each and every day! As you develop the discipline of being in God's Word on a daily basis, our prayer is that you will fall in love with Him even more as you spend time reading from the Bible.

Each day before you read the assigned scripture(s), pray and ask God to help you understand it. Invite Him to speak to you through His Word. Then listen. It's His job to speak to you, and it's your job to listen and obey.

Take time to read the verses over and over again. We are told in Proverbs to search and you will find: "Search for it like silver, and hunt for it like hidden treasure. Then you will understand" (Prov. 2:4–5 NCV).

We are thrilled to provide these different resources for you as you participate in our online Bible study:

- *You Are Forgiven* Study Book
- Reading Plan
- Weekly Blog Posts (Mondays, Wednesdays, and Fridays)
- Weekly Memory Verses
- Weekly Monday Videos
- Weekly Challenges
- Online Community:
  Facebook, Twitter, Instagram, LoveGodGreatly.com
- Hashtags: #LoveGodGreatly

All of us here at Love God Greatly can't wait for you to get started, and we hope to see you at the finish line. Endure, persevere, press on—and don't give up! Finish well what you are beginning today. We will be here every step of the way, cheering you on! We are in this together. Fight to rise early, to push back the stress of the day, to sit alone and spend time in God's Word! Let's see what God has in store for you in this study! Journey with us as we learn to love God greatly with our lives!

Our Community

LOVE GOD GREATLY (LGG) is a beautiful community of women who use a variety of technology platforms to keep each other accountable in God's Word.

We start with a simple Bible reading plan, but it doesn't stop there.

Some women gather in homes and churches locally, while others connect online with women across the globe. Whatever the method, we lovingly lock arms and unite for this purpose: to love God greatly with our lives.

In today's fast-paced technology-driven world, it would be easy to study God's Word in an isolated environment that lacks encouragement or support, but that isn't the intention here at Love God Greatly. God created us to live in community with Him and with those around us.

We need each other, and we live life better together.

Because of this, would you consider reaching out and doing this study with someone?

All of us have women in our lives who need friendship, accountability, and have the desire to dive into God's Word on a deeper level. Rest assured we'll be studying right alongside you—learning with you, cheering for you, enjoying sweet fellowship, and smiling from ear to ear as we watch God unite women together—intentionally connecting hearts and minds for His glory.

It's pretty unreal, this opportunity we have to grow not only closer to God through this study but also to each other. So here's the challenge: call your mom, your sister, your grandma, the girl across the street, or the college friend across the country. Gather a group of girls from your church or workplace, or meet in a coffee shop with friends you have always wished you knew better. Utilize the beauty of connecting online for inspiration and accountability, and take opportunities to meet in person when you can.

Arm-in-arm and hand-in-hand, let's do this thing…together.

How to SOAP

WE'RE PROUD OF YOU.

We really want you to know that.

We're proud of you for making the commitment to be in God's Word, to be reading it each day and applying it to your life, the beautiful life our Lord has given you.

In this study we offer you a study journal to accompany the verses we are reading. This journal is designed to help you interact with God's Word and learn to dig deeper, encouraging you to slow down and reflect on what God is saying to you that day.

At Love God Greatly, we use the SOAP Bible study method. Before beginning, let's take a moment to define this method and share why we recommend using it during your quiet time.

Why SOAP It?

It's one thing to simply read Scripture. But when you interact with it, intentionally slowing down to really reflect on it, suddenly words start popping off the page. The SOAP method allows you to dig deeper into Scripture and see more than you would if you simply read the verses and then went on your merry way. Please take the time to SOAP through our Bible studies and see for yourself how much more you get from your daily reading. You'll be amazed.

What Does SOAP Mean?

S stands for **Scripture**. Physically write out the verses. You'll be amazed at what God will reveal to you just by taking the time to slow down and write out what you are reading!

O stands for **observation**. What do you see in the verses that you're reading? Who is the intended audience? Is there a repetition of words? What words stand out to you?

A stands for **application**. This is when God's Word becomes personal. What is God saying to you today? How can you apply what you just read to your own personal life? What changes do you need to make? Is there action you need to take?

P stands for **prayer**. Pray God's Word back to Him. Spend time thanking Him. If He has revealed something to you during this time in His Word, pray about it. If He has revealed some sin that is in your life, confess. And remember, He loves you dearly.

Follow This Example

Scripture: Read and write out Colossians 1:5–8.

> "The faith and love that spring from the hope stored up for you in heaven and about which you have already heard in the true message of the gospel that has come to you. In the same way, the gospel is bearing fruit and growing throughout the whole world— just as it has been doing among you since the day you heard it and truly understood God's grace. You learned it from Epaphras, our dear fellow servant, who is a faithful minister of Christ on our behalf, and who also told us of your love in the Spirit" (NIV).

Observation: Write what stands out to you.

> When you combine faith and love, you get hope. We must remember that our hope is in heaven; it is yet to come. The gospel is the Word of truth. The gospel is continually bearing fruit and growing from the first day to the last. It just takes one person to change a whole community...Epaphras.

Application: Apply this scripture to your own life.

God used one man, Epaphras, to change a whole town. I was reminded that we are simply called to tell others about Christ; it's God's job to spread the gospel, to grow it, and have it bear fruit. I felt today's verses were almost directly spoken to Love God Greatly women: "The gospel is bearing fruit and growing throughout the whole world—just as it has been doing among you since the day you heard it and truly understood God's grace."

It's so fun when God's Word comes alive and encourages us in our current situation! My passionate desire is that all the women involved in our LGG Bible study will understand God's grace and have a thirst for His Word. I was moved by this quote from my Bible commentary today: "God's Word is not just for our information, it is for our transformation."

Prayer: Pray over this.

Dear Lord, please help me to be an "Epaphras," to tell others about You and then leave the results in Your loving hands. Please help me to understand and apply personally what I have read today to my life, thereby becoming more and more like You each and every day. Help me to live a life that bears the fruit of faith and love, anchoring my hope in heaven, not here on earth. Help me to remember that the best is yet to come!

SOAP It Up

Remember, the most important ingredients in the SOAP method are your interaction with God's Word and your application of His Word to your life:

Blessed is the one who does not walk in step with the wicked or stand in the way that sinners take or sit in the company of mockers, but whose delight is in the law of the LORD, and who meditates on his law day and night. That person is like a tree planted by streams of water, which yields its fruit in season and whose leaf does not wither—whatever they do prospers. (Ps. 1:1–3, NIV)

Reading Plan

		Read	SOAP
WEEK 1	Monday	Isaiah 59:1-5	Isaiah 59:2
	Tuesday	Ephesians 2:1-3, 12	Ephesians 2:12
	Wednesday	John 8:31-34	John 8:34
	Thursday	Jeremiah 17:9	Jeremiah 17:9
	Friday	Romans 7:18-19	Romans 7:18
	Response Day		
WEEK 2	Monday	Ephesians 1:3-7	Ephesians 1:7
	Tuesday	John 3:16-21	John 3:16
	Wednesday	Luke 13:1-5	Luke 13:5
	Thursday	John 1:26-30	John 1:29
	Friday	2 Chronicles 7:12-16	2 Chronicles 7:14
	Response Day		
WEEK 3	Monday	1 John 1:5-9	1 John 1:9
	Tuesday	Micah 7:18-19	Micah 7:19
	Wednesday	Hebrews 9:23-28	Hebrews 9:28
	Thursday	Psalm 103:11-13	Psalm 103:12
	Friday	Isaiah 38:17-19	Isaiah 38:17
	Response Day		
WEEK 4	Monday	2 Corinthians 5	2 Corinthians 5:17
	Tuesday	Romans 12:1-2	Romans 12:2
	Wednesday	Romans 6:1-10	Romans 6:6
	Thursday	Colossians 3:1-17	Colossians 3:1-3
	Friday	1 John 5:1-4	1 John 5:4
	Response Day		
WEEK 5	Monday	Colossians 3:12-14	Colossians 3:13
	Tuesday	Matthew 18:21-35	Matthew 18:21-22
	Wednesday	Romans 12:17-21	Romans 12:21
	Thursday	Mark 11:20-25	Mark 11:25
	Friday	Matthew 6:9-13	Matthew 6:12-13
	Response Day		
WEEK 6	Monday	Psalm 103	Psalm 103:10-11
	Tuesday	1 Corinthians 15:50-57	1 Corinthians 15:57
	Wednesday	Luke 17:11-19	Luke 17:15-16
	Thursday	Psalm 118:20-24	Psalm 118:21
	Friday	Ephesians 5:20	Ephesians 5:20
	Response Day		
WEEK 7	Monday	1 Corinthians 13:4-13	1 Corinthians 13:4-5
	Tuesday	1 John 4:7-11	1 John 4:7
	Wednesday	John 13:34-35	John 13:34
	Thursday	Isaiah 61:10-11	Isaiah 61:10
	Friday	Habakkuk 3:17-19	Habakkuk 3:18-19
	Response Day		
WEEK 8	Monday	2 Corinthians 5:18-19	2 Corinthians 5:18-19
	Tuesday	Matthew 28:16-20	Matthew 28:19-20
	Wednesday	Isaiah 52:6-8	Isaiah 52:7
	Thursday	Romans 10:10-15	Romans 10:14-15
	Friday	Matthew 9:35-38	Matthew 9:37-38
	Response Day		

Goals

WE BELIEVE it's important to write out goals for this study. Take some time now and write three goals you would like to focus on as you begin to rise each day and dig into God's Word. Make sure and refer back to these goals throughout the next eight weeks to help you stay focused. You can do it!

My goals are:

1.

2.

3.

Signature: _____

Date: _____

Introduction

DO YOU OWN A cross necklace or have a decorative cross hanging somewhere in your home? I do. Many of us wear crosses around our necks, on our ears, or as rings on our fingers. Maybe you have a cross tattoo. I have a set of candles with crosses on them. The cross has become not only a symbol of the sacrifice made by Jesus Christ but also a mainstream symbol of religion and simple spirituality.

For too many, all these crosses carry a superficial sentiment. It doesn't move us like it should. Even the decorative cross hanging in my living room does not move me to tears because of Christ's sacrifice or my guilt. It should. But I bought it at Hobby Lobby because it looked pretty. It is easy to forget what the cross is truly all about.

And on the other end of this spectrum are those who have placed too much emphasis on the cross as an object. Throughout history many have sought out pieces of the "true" cross of Christ. Way back in AD 326 the Empress Helena (the mother of Constantine) began to search for Christ's tomb and the place of Golgotha. As the story goes, Helena ended up finding three crosses, which she believed to have been the cross of Christ as well as those used to execute the two thieves who hung next to Jesus. Like those who miss the significance of the cross in light of its popular artistic merit, so some have missed its significance by looking for the wood it was made of.

How was Helena going to figure out which one of the three crosses actually held the body of Jesus? A couple different stories are recorded. One says there was a prominent woman in the city who was terminally ill. One by one the crosses were brought to her. The first two crosses did nothing, but when the nearly dead woman touched the third cross she was instantly healed.[1]

Throughout the years many have made pilgrimages to see, touch, and kiss an alleged part of the "real cross" in order to be healed and receive blessing. Sadly, many have turned the cross into an idol, believing that the wooden cross beams had special powers. The instrument of torture, for many, became something to trust in apart from Jesus Christ.

But the cross is not a trinket we can put on and take off. Nor is it just an example of suffering and obedience. It is not a relic filled with healing power. It is not merely a beautiful piece of decoration. The cross is not a talisman that will bring us good luck and blessings.

The truth is, whether or not the cross on which Jesus died still exists is irrelevant. A piece of wood holds no power. The cross was a device of torture on which the Son of God secured for us the eternal forgiveness of God the Father: "God made you alive with Christ, and he forgave all our sins. He canceled the debt, which listed all the rules we failed to follow. He took away that record with its rules and nailed it to the cross" (Col. 2:13–14 NCV).

The cross itself is not our hope. What Jesus did on the cross is what saves all who believe. On the cross Jesus made satisfaction of God's wrath.

On the cross Jesus made payment of our ransom. On the cross Jesus was punished for our sins.

On the cross Jesus destroyed the power of sin and the curse of death.

And on the cross Jesus ensured forgiveness for those who believe in Him.

This is what our study is all about: how Jesus obtained for us the forgiveness of sins by his death.

In this study we will examine many of the different facets of forgiveness. Why do we need it? How do we get it? What is the extent of our forgiveness, and how should it change us?

The cross is precious because on it our Savior poured out His life for us. We received pardon and the power to forgive others. Forgiveness is our treasure, but we can't hang forgiveness on our walls or drape it around our necks. Instead, we use the cross as a reminder of the beautiful gift of forgiveness Christ gave to us.

---

1 Jan Willem Drijvers, Helena Augusta, Brill Academic Publishers, October 1, 1991. [Leiden]

You are
FORGIVEN

Week 1

Week 1 Challenge (Note: You can find this listed in our Monday blog post):

Prayer focus for this week: Spend time praying for your family members.

Praying	Praise
Monday	
Tuesday	
Wednesday	
Thursday	
Friday	

"Your iniquities have made a separation between you and your God, and your sins have hidden his face from you so that he does not hear".

ISAIAH 59:2

Scripture for Week 1

MONDAY   ISAIAH 59:1-5 (ESV)

^{59} Behold, the Lord's hand is not shortened, that it cannot save,
   or his ear dull, that it cannot hear;
^{2} but your iniquities have made a separation
   between you and your God,
and your sins have hidden his face from you
   so that he does not hear.
^{3} For your hands are defiled with blood
   and your fingers with iniquity;
your lips have spoken lies;
   your tongue mutters wickedness.
^{4} No one enters suit justly;
   no one goes to law honestly;
they rely on empty pleas, they speak lies,
   they conceive mischief and give birth to iniquity.
^{5} They hatch adders' eggs;
   they weave the spider's web;
he who eats their eggs dies,
   and from one that is crushed a viper is hatched.

TUESDAY   EPHESIANS 2:1-3 (ESV)

^{2} And you were dead in the trespasses and sins ^{2} in which you once walked, following the course of this world, following the prince of the power of the air, the spirit that is now at work in the sons of disobedience— ^{3} among whom we all once lived in the passions of our flesh, carrying out the desires of the body and the mind, and were by nature children of wrath, like the rest of mankind.

EPHESIANS 2:12 (ESV)

¹² remember that you were at that time separated from Christ, alienated from the commonwealth of Israel and strangers to the covenants of promise, having no hope and without God in the world.

WEDNESDAY   *JOHN 8:31-34 (ESV)*

³¹ So Jesus said to the Jews who had believed him, "If you abide in my word, you are truly my disciples, ³² and you will know the truth, and the truth will set you free." ³³ They answered him, "We are offspring of Abraham and have never been enslaved to anyone. How is it that you say, 'You will become free'?"

³⁴ Jesus answered them, "Truly, truly, I say to you, everyone who practices sin is a slave to sin.

THURSDAY   *JEREMIAH 17:9 (ESV)*

⁹ The heart is deceitful above all things,

and desperately sick;

who can understand it?

FRIDAY   *ROMANS 7:18-19 (ESV)*

¹⁸ For I know that nothing good dwells in me, that is, in my flesh. For I have the desire to do what is right, but not the ability to carry it out. ¹⁹ For I do not do the good I want, but the evil I do not want is what I keep on doing.

1

THE NEED FOR FORGIVENESS

BY JEN THORN

A Changed Heart

HISTORY IS FILLED with stories of people who were terribly wronged but were still able to extend the hand of forgiveness. One amazing example is that of Robert Rule.

In 2003 Gary Leon Ridgway, also known as the Green River Killer, was convicted of raping, choking and then murdering 48 women. At the sentencing the families of these senseless killings had the opportunity to say a few words to Gary Ridgway. All of them were overflowing with grief, and many were filled with anger. Some told him that he was a monster, and others told him that he belonged in hell. But one man, Robert Rule, whose teenage daughter had been killed by this insane man, had other words. He said, "Mr. Ridgeway, there are people here who hate you. I'm not one of them. You've made it very difficult to live up to what I believe, and that is what God says to do, and that's to forgive. You are forgiven, sir."

It took the power of Christ's blood to not only forgive Mr. Rule of his sins, but to make it possible for him to extend forgiveness to a man who so coldly took the life of his daughter.

We are excited to write a book on the life-changing forgiveness we have in Jesus Christ. Many of us have grown so accustomed to the reality of our forgiveness that it does not ignite the love, passion, and thanksgiving it once did. The excitement has worn off, and we feel a bit cold in our walk with God. We hope that through this book our awe for what God has done for us will be rekindled. We want to know forgiveness deeply and want to help others see it for what it truly is. In this book we will look at forgiveness from a number of different angles. But in order to fully understand forgiveness, we must look at why we need to be forgiven in the first place. How did we get into this mess called sin, and why can't we get out of it ourselves?

Let's start at the beginning.

Why We Need Forgiveness

Adam and Eve were the world's first couple. Actually they were the world's first (and only) *perfect* couple whose home was unpolluted and untouched by anything but goodness and purity. No angry words were exchanged between husband and wife, no sighs of impatience, no annoyed eye rolling, and no discontentment. Eve did not complain about Adam not picking up after himself and Adam didn't mind Eve telling him *all* about her day. Their relationship was sweet and kind, fun and fulfilling. They were loving toward each other, of one mind, and in perfect fellowship with the God who made them. They were sinless.

This is really hard to imagine, isn't it? We look at the world and our lives as they are now and see a twisted version of how it was meant to be. Selfishness and hate dominate. We struggle daily to beat down the sin that wants to take over. We snap at our spouse, yell at the kids, and are rude to strangers. We offend easily and are easily offended. We are quick to bear a grudge and slow to forgive. We mistreat creation, take for granted the gifts we have, and ignore the God who is our hope. Like the prophet Isaiah said, all of us have gone our own way (Isa. 53:6). How did we become so unlike our first parents?

Because of Our Parents

The truth is, we look exactly like Adam and Eve after they themselves broke fellowship with God and each other by choosing to sin (Gen. 3). Satan, the great enemy of God, the despiser of Jesus, and the hater of God's people, used his quiet and devious ways to plant doubt and lies in the minds of our first parents. And in the midst of temptation, instead of running to their heavenly Father, they were willing to listen and then act upon the devil's lies. Eve fell first, then her husband, and with them the whole created order fell into sin. The fall of this couple affected the rest of humanity, tainting every human that ever lived and will ever live. Gone were the days of perfect peace and unity. Perfect love and understanding were suddenly a thing of the past. Selflessness and generosity warped into selfishness and greed.

"In the first garden, 'Not Your will but mine' (by Adam) changed Paradise to desert and brought mankind from Eden to Gethsemane. Now 'Not My will but Yours' (by Jesus Christ) brings anguish to the man who prays it but transforms the desert into the kingdom and brings man from Gethsemane to the gates of glory."[1]

We have received a terrible gift from our first earthly father, Adam. From him we have received what theologians call "original sin." Original sin is made up of two parts: an imputed guilt and an inherited sinful nature. Stick with me here, because these are important concepts for us to understand.

Imputed Sin

First, when Adam sinned in the garden not only did he become guilty as a sinner, but we, too, became guilty with him. Adam represented us all, and as the head of the human race, when he sinned, we all sinned. Don't miss this. When Adam sinned, somehow we all sinned with him.

Therefore, just as sin came into the world through one man, and death through sin, death spread to all men because all sinned (Rom. 5:12). Pastor Sam Storms said, "Remember this: only if Adam represents you in the Garden can Jesus represent you on Golgotha. It was on the cross that Jesus served as your representative head: His obedience to the law, His righteousness, His suffering the penalty of the law, were all the acts of a covenant head acting in the stead and on behalf of His people. If Adam stood for you in the Garden, Christ may also hang for you on the cross."[2]

1 D. A. Carson. *"Matthew, The Expositor's Bible Commentary."* Zondervan. 1984. p. 545.
2 Sam Storms. *"Original Sin and Total Depravity, Part 1."* SamStorms.com. Enjoying God

Adam's guilt is our guilt. This is the first half of our need for forgiveness.

Inherited Sin

The second aspect of original sin is the human nature we inherited from Adam. Adam changed when he sinned in the garden. His very nature changed, becoming corrupt. From that moment on, Adam struggled with doing right, and in all he did, sin was right there with him. As the father of all people, he passed down to all of us his sinful nature. This is why we say, do, and think sinful things. We don't have to be taught how to sin; it is part of our very nature. This has left us all in a state of unrighteousness.

As it is written, "None is righteous, no, not one" (Rom. 3:10).

Adam's nature is our nature. This is the second half of our need for forgiveness.

According to author John Piper, "So we have seen two things that need a remedy. One is our sinful nature that enslaves us to sin, and the other is our original guilt and condemnation that is rooted not first in our individual sinning but in our connection with Adam in his sin."[3]

Both of these aspects of our sin are important for us to grasp, because it shows us the mess we are in and should give us a glimpse of our utter helplessness and our desperate need for a Savior. It leaves no room for us saving ourselves, because our sin goes too deep. Sin has affected every part of who we are. It has blackened our heart, twisted our will, and poisoned our soul.

The consequences of our sin are tragic. It has created a chasm between us and God that is so great it is impossible for man to build a bridge across it. Sometimes we try. We try by being good, cleaning ourselves up, loving others, being charitable, attempting to obey the Ten Commandments, reading our Bible, or going to church. We believe that this will bridge the gap between us and God, that somehow our efforts will earn God's favor. But God requires perfection and purity (1 Peter. 1:16), and our efforts fall short: "Your iniquities have made a separation between you and your God, and your sins have hidden his face from you so that he does not hear" (Isa. 59:2).

Who needs to be forgiven? Sinners. That's all of us. We are guilty for

Ministries. Web. 28 June 2016.
3 John Piper, Desiring God blog post, *"Adam, Christ, and Justification,"* V, 2000. DesiringGod.org

what happened in the garden, and guilty for the actions we have committed in the few decades we have on this earth. Our problem is not just what we have done, but what we have become.

Theologian R. C. Sproul said, "We are not sinners because we sin; rather, we sin because we are sinners."[4]

We Need Forgiveness Because of our Hearts

Humanity's common perception is that people are basically good. Sure there are always bad examples, but we also see examples of kindness, compassion, love, sacrifice, and generosity. How can we consider people of good reputation and conduct "bad"?

We have to start with the true measure of goodness. The measure of our goodness is not found in the actions of individuals. The goodness we see in humanity today is relative—good only in comparison to other human beings. And when we see it, we are at best seeing the vestiges of the image of God in us. What we don't always see is what lies beneath our good deeds. Our best works are imperfect, falling short of God's standards, and are often mixed with motives that are not aimed at God's glory and the good of others. Sometimes we simply do what is right because we know we should. Sometimes we do what is good because we feel we have to or because we know it will make us look good. Our sin problem is not external but internal. Sin touches our very core, and the effect sin has on our hearts is devastating. Its poison has sunk in and has petrified our hearts, turning them to stone (Ezek. 36:26).

The Bible has harsh things to say about the condition of our hearts. They can be painful to read and hard to accept, but because these are the words of God, we must believe them in order to know who we are and what we really need. Such understanding will also create in us an awe and thankfulness that the God whom we have offended and railed against should go to great lengths to save us. Scripture has these things to say about the condition of our hearts:

> The heart is deceitful above all things, and desperately sick; who can understand it? (Jer. 17:9)

4 R. C. Sproul, *God's Love: How the Infinite God Cares for His Children*, 2012. David C. Cook Publishing.

Out of the heart come evil thoughts, murder, adultery, sexual immorality, theft, false witness, slander. (Matt. 15:19)

Then the Lord saw that the wickedness of man was great on the earth, and that every intent of the thoughts of his heart was only evil continually. (Gen. 6:5)

What all of this means is that in the heart, the very center of our being, is where our corruption is found. The human heart is the birthplace for all our sins. Protestant Reformer John Calvin said the human heart is like an idol factory, always churning out new idols to worship.[5] And John Owen, a Puritan pastor in the 1600s, called the human heart a "hornet's nest of evil."[6]

Let me be clear, this does not mean we are as sinful or as wicked as we could possibly be, nor does it mean that people are without a knowledge of right and wrong, without a conscience, or self-control of some kind. What it does mean is that all our works are tainted with sin. We have nothing to offer God that is not smeared somehow with the dirt of corruption. The stain of sin is on us and everything we do, no matter how good those things appear to be.

The spiritually dead have stony hearts that do not beat with true love for God and neighbor. Instead, we often create a god of our own liking and in our own image. We bristle and get upset at some of the things that God tells us in His word. And we run from the extreme of hating people to idolizing them to feeling totally indifferent about people's condition and need. This is what spiritual death looks like. We are dead to God. And that is why we all need forgiveness.

Proverbs asks the important question, "Who can say, 'I made my heart pure; I am clean from my sin?'" (Prov. 20:9). The answer, of course, is no one! It is only when we begin to see the depth of our need that we can begin to see the greatness of God's love for us in Jesus Christ.

---

5 John Calvin. *Institutes of the Christian Religion.* Revised Edition 1986. Wm. B. Eerdmans Publishing Company.
6 Jeff Robinson. *"8 Reasons We Need the Puritans."* Web log post. TGC. N.p., n.d. Web. 12 July 2016.

We Need Forgiveness Because of Our Actions

All of us can think back over our life and see the sins we have committed. From our earliest days on earth, sin has been our close companion. We have all been stingy and unjustly angry. We have used our words to hurt people and withhold truth. We have gossiped and slandered. We have been proud and put ourselves before God and others.

As children we have fought with our siblings and friends, lied to our parents, and cheated in school. When my husband was in third grade he and his friend vandalized a church. I remember taking some money out of my mom's purse in order to buy some candy on my way home from school. From what we consider "small" sins to the "big" sins, all of it makes the youngest of us worthy of God's just judgment.

But sin stays with us as we grow. It grows with us, and our ability to sin matures. Some of us may have done terrible things in our adult years that make us cringe when we think about them. The pain we have inflicted on others can make us feel shameful even now. Some may have done things that have yielded serious consequences that we continue to experience to this very day. No matter how moral we think we are or have been, we all have lived lives littered with sin and corruption.

The only escape for our corruption and condemnation is through the life and death of Jesus Christ. God's just anger has been appeased by the precious blood of our Savior who was the sacrifice needed to bridge the chasm between us and God. We are no longer under condemnation (Rom. 8:1), and God is no longer against us but for us (Rom 8). But, while sin's penalty has been removed, its presence continues in our lives.

Simul Justus et Peccator. This Latin phrase is tattooed across my husband's chest. It means "simultaneously justified and sinful" and is a reminder to him that he, as a Christian, is at the same time a sinner and a saint. Martin Luther used this phrase in the 1500s to speak to the truth that even as Christians, who have been reconciled to God, sin still clings to us, leaving us in a state needing God continually.

We can all lament with Paul when he said, "For I do not do the good I want, but the evil I do not want is what I keep on doing" (Rom. 7:19). We all understand his frustration. But this frustration is actually a good sign. It means we have been changed, that our hearts now love what God loves and hates what God hates. No, not perfectly, but we desire to be godly and to do good, and we hate the sin we see in our lives. These are signs of a changed heart.

God has taken our heart of stone and turned it into a heart of flesh, a heart that beats with love for our God. Yet sin is still alive in us. What we tend to forget is that we have been set free from the power of that remaining sin. We can fight against it and we can win, because we now have the power of the Holy Spirit residing within each one of us. And as sin remains with us, we can pray confidently, "Forgive us our sins" (Luke 11:4) with the assurance that as we confess our sins God is faithful and just to forgive us and cleanse us from all unrighteousness (1 John 1:9).

Seventeenth-century theologian John Flavel asked, did Christ finish His work for us? Yes! So there's no doubt but He will also finish His work in us.[7]

Our greatest need in life is not money, family, or friendship. It isn't even food and water, as critical as those are for this life. Our greatest need is to be forgiven of our sins and reconciled to the God we have sinned against. We are all guilty sinners because of our first parents, our hearts, and our actions. But the grace of God is bigger than our sins, and His forgiveness is able to cover all of it. It covers every law we have broken in our past, every command we have transgressed in the present, and every commandment we will disobey in the future. The forgiving grace of God removes our guilt entirely and enables us to live in freedom under the love and acceptance of God.

The apostle Paul's letter to the Ephesians reminds us: "Remember that you were at that time separated from Christ, alienated from the commonwealth of Israel and strangers to the covenants of promise, having no hope and without God in the world. But now in Christ Jesus you who once were far off have been brought near by the blood of Christ" (Eph. 2:12–13).

---

7 John Flavel, *Fountain of Life: A Display of Christ in His Essential and Mediatorial Glory*, 1836. W. Baynes and Son.

PRAYER

Heavenly Father, thank You for showing us the need for forgiveness. Thank You for making a way for us to be forgiven and cleansed of our sins through Your Son, Jesus Christ. May we be obedient to extend forgiveness to others in keeping with Your commands and be quick to remember that You have taken our heart of stone and turned it into a heart of flesh, a heart that beats with love for our God. In Jesus' name. Amen.

SHEILA'S TESTIMONY

It started out as a normal day in the life of a teenager. I had no idea when I woke up that morning that on this day my life would be forever changed. Upon arriving home from school, the telephone began to ring. Like a typical fifteen- year-old, I ran to answer the phone. It was a neighbor calling to say that my dad was in an accident at work and was hurt. It wasn't long before my grandfather arrived at the house and said I needed to go with him.

Before nightfall, my father died. Dad was a junior blaster on a coal-stripping job, and the man who normally did that job had taken off that day and Dad had taken his place. My heart began to fill with such anger, and a hatred for that man built inside me. I became bitter, and that bitterness rooted deep into my heart. I was not a Christian and knew nothing of forgiveness, mercy, or real love. All I knew was I was fifteen and my father was gone forever because someone called off work. It should not have been my dad that died.

The anger grew inside me. I began drinking, partying, hanging out with friends, and ditching school until I finally dropped out. I ended up married at the age of seventeen. My life became one bad choice after another. It's been said, "bitterness is taking poison and waiting for the other person to die." My anger, rage, and unforgiveness had become a deeply entrenched bitter root.

Although I got very good at appearances, my unresolved hatred for this man had filled me utterly and completely.

In the ensuing years I birthed two wonderful boys who I might say are my whole world. I completed my GED and even went to college. But through it all, the intensity of my hatred for the man only grew. Years passed and I divorced.

In time, I remarried and that is when my journey to forgiveness and healing began. My husband found a church and we began attending regularly. I gave my heart to Jesus, and slowly, week after week, my heart began to soften. The more I felt the love of our new church family, the more I began to understand the love of God.

One day my husband and I were talking about my unresolved bitterness and he said, "It's time to forgive him." I was reluctant at first, but I felt a tug in my heart that was agreeing with him. I will never forget the process that took place that day, when God used my husband to lead me toward a place of forgiveness.

We talked and I cried. My husband urged me to make a verbal profession of forgiveness. I hesitated, but then I audibly said I forgave the man. I said it again and again and again. Suddenly it was as though I could see that man and the burden he was carrying, knowing that it would have been him that died instead of my father. It was as though God was showing me his family, his wife, his children. My heart broke into pieces for ever wishing this pain upon another person.

That was the beginning of freedom for me. For years I looked through the lens of my loss: my dad missing my growing up, missing my wedding day, the birth of my sons, my graduation from college. I had viewed my life from a self-focused perspective, but now it was as if God was allowing me to look at this man and his family in a new and different way.

I verbally forgave the man, and the feelings slowly followed. It was some time before the thought of him didn't provoke negative emotions, but the day did come. Two years ago I came face-to-face with him, and he had no idea who I was.

I remember looking at him, and at that moment feeling whole. No longer did I want to spew out all my pain upon him. My heart flooded with the thought that I no longer carried any ill feelings, hatred, or contempt for him. I truly had forgiven him.

I thanked God that day, not only for releasing me from the bondage of unforgiveness, but also for this man's life. I thanked God that his children had a father to watch them grow up and that he was able to have a full life with his family. Ahh. I was free. God's grace, mercy, and love now filled those deep places where that bitter root of unforgiveness once held my heart captive.

- - - - - - - - -

It is for freedom that Christ has set us free. Stand firm, then, and do not let yourselves be burdened again by a yoke of slavery.

(Gal. 5:1 NIV)

Monday

READ: Isaiah 59:1-5
SOAP: Isaiah 59:2

Scripture - Write out the **Scripture** passage for the day.

Observations - Write down 1 or 2 **observations** from the passage.

Monday

Applications - Write down 1 or 2 **applications** from the passage.

Pray - Write out a **prayer** over what you learned from today's passage.

-Visit our website today for the corresponding blog post!-

Tuesday

READ: Ephesians 2:1-3, 12
SOAP: Ephesians 2:12

Scripture - Write out the **Scripture** passage for the day.

Observations - Write down 1 or 2 **observations** from the passage.

Tuesday

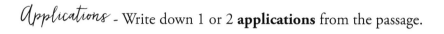

Applications - Write down 1 or 2 **applications** from the passage.

Pray - Write out a **prayer** over what you learned from today's passage.

Wednesday

READ: John 8:31-34
SOAP: John 8:34

Scripture - Write out the **Scripture** passage for the day.

Observations - Write down 1 or 2 **observations** from the passage.

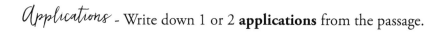

Wednesday

Applications - Write down 1 or 2 **applications** from the passage.

Pray - Write out a **prayer** over what you learned from today's passage.

-Visit our website today for the corresponding blog post!-

Thursday

READ: Jeremiah 17:9
SOAP: Jeremiah 17:9

Scripture - Write out the **Scripture** passage for the day.

Observations - Write down 1 or 2 **observations** from the passage.

Thursday

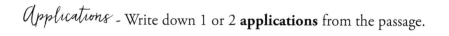

Applications - Write down 1 or 2 **applications** from the passage.

Pray - Write out a **prayer** over what you learned from today's passage.

Friday

READ: Romans 7:18-19
SOAP: Romans 7:18

Scripture - Write out the **Scripture** passage for the day.

Observations - Write down 1 or 2 **observations** from the passage.

Friday

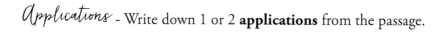

Applications - Write down 1 or 2 **applications** from the passage.

Pray - Write out a **prayer** over what you learned from today's passage.

-Visit our website today for the corresponding blog post!-

Reflection Questions

1. Define for yourself the difference between imputed sin and inherited sin, and consider why both of these aspects of our sin make Jesus' ultimate sacrifice necessary.

2. What "good works" do you do in an attempt to atone for the sin in your life?

3. Prayerfully ask God if there is someone you need to forgive, someone from whom you have previously withheld your forgiveness?

4. Has someone ever hurt you or a loved one so badly that you wished them ill? What do you think Jesus would want you to do with those feelings?

5. What role does the Holy Spirit play in your ability to forgive?

My Response

Week 2

Week 2 Challenge (Note: You can find this listed in our Monday blog post):

Prayer focus for this week: Spend time praying for your country.

Praying	Praise
Monday	
Tuesday	
Wednesday	
Thursday	
Friday	

"In him we have
redemption through his blood,
the forgiveness of sins,
in accordance with the
riches of God's grace".

EPHESIANS 1:7

Scripture for Week 2

MONDAY

EPHESIANS 1:3-7 (ESV)

3 Blessed be the God and Father of our Lord Jesus Christ, who has blessed us in Christ with every spiritual blessing in the heavenly places, 4 even as he chose us in him before the foundation of the world, that we should be holy and blameless before him. In love 5 he predestined us for adoption as sons through Jesus Christ, according to the purpose of his will, 6 to the praise of his glorious grace, with which he has blessed us in the Beloved. 7 In him we have redemption through his blood, the forgiveness of our trespasses, according to the riches of his grace,

TUESDAY

JOHN 3:16-21 (ESV)

16 "For God so loved the world, that he gave his only Son, that whoever believes in him should not perish but have eternal life. 17 For God did not send his Son into the world to condemn the world, but in order that the world might be saved through him. 18 Whoever believes in him is not condemned, but whoever does not believe is condemned already, because he has not believed in the name of the only Son of God. 19 And this is the judgment:the light has come into the world, and people loved the darkness rather than the light because their works were evil. 20 For everyone who does wicked things hates the light and does not come to the light, lest his works should be exposed. 21 But whoever does what is true comes to the light, so that it may be clearly seen that his works have been carried out in God."

WEDNESDAY

LUKE 13:1-5 (ESV)

13 There were some present at that very time who told him about the Galileans whose bloodPilate had mingled with their sacrifices. 2 And he answered them, "Do you think that these Galileans were worse sinners than all the other Galileans, because they suffered

in this way?³ No, I tell you; but unless you repent, you will all likewise perish. ⁴ Or those eighteen on whom the tower in Siloam fell and killed them: do you think that they were worse offenders than all the others who lived in Jerusalem? ⁵ No, I tell you; but unless you repent, you will all likewise perish."

THURSDAY   *JOHN 1:26-30 (ESV)*

²⁶ John answered them, "I baptize with water, but among you stands one you do not know,²⁷ even he who comes after me, the strap of whose sandal I am not worthy to untie." ²⁸ These things took place in Bethany across the Jordan, where John was baptizing.

²⁹ The next day he saw Jesus coming toward him, and said, "Behold, the Lamb of God, who takes away the sin of the world! ³⁰ This is he of whom I said, 'After me comes a man who ranks before me, because he was before me.'

FRIDAY   *2 CHRONICLES 7:12-16 (ESV)*

¹² Then the Lord appeared to Solomon in the night and said to him: "I have heard your prayer and have chosen this place for myself as a house of sacrifice. ¹³ When I shut up the heavens so that there is no rain, or command the locust to devour the land, or send pestilence among my people, ¹⁴ if my people who are called by my name humble themselves, and pray and seek my face and turn from their wicked ways, then I will hear from heaven and will forgive their sin and heal their land. ¹⁵ Now my eyes will be open and my ears attentive to the prayer that is made in this place. ¹⁶ For now I have chosen and consecrated this house that my name may be there forever. My eyes and my heart will be there for all time.

2

THE WAY OF FORGIVENESS

BY WHITNEY DAUGHERTY

"Forgiveness. Nothing is more foreign to sinful nature. And nothing is more characteristic of divine grace."

—John MacArthur

"God so loved the world, that he gave his only Son, that whoever believes in him should not perish but have eternal life" (John 3:16).

The Cover-Up

THE NEW DAY PEEKED in through the windows, lighting up the sun-yellow painted walls of my childhood bedroom. Man, I loved that bedroom, especially the bright butterfly wallpaper that accented one wall. It was hard to enter that chipper room and not find joy, even on the gloomiest of days.

The sun was up. However, I was not. And in stark contrast to the cheerful decor, any glimmer of happiness had long left the building.

Oh, I was awake, awake and sweaty from the steaming sauna created by my warm breath beneath the pile of bedcovers. My seven-year-old lanky self was buried underneath from head to toe, and I distinctly remember taking quiet, shallow breaths in an attempt to disguise my location. I mustered a simple prayer, begging God to convince the rest of the house—most importantly anyone with the title of "parent"—that I was still sleeping. Maybe, just maybe, I could fool them. They'd walk on by like nothing had ever happened, and I wouldn't have to face the consequences for my disobedience the night before.

It didn't take long for me to realize I couldn't fake it forever. This cover-up operation wasn't fooling anyone, especially not me. In fact, I was only becoming more miserable by the minute. No matter what painstaking measures I took to hide, the blankets placed strategically over my head would never cover up the offenses that were buried deep down in my heart.

We Conceal

From the very beginning, it's been human nature to cover up our sin. Adam and Eve set the stage early on in the garden, and we've been following in their footsteps ever since: "They heard the sound of the LORD God walking in the garden in the cool of the day, and the man and his wife *hid themselves* from the presence of the LORD God among the trees of the garden" (Gen. 3:8, emphasis mine). As a young child, it was intuitive for me to hide under those covers. I don't even have an immense recollection of early childhood memories, but I'll never forget the emotions and determination behind my hiding that day. In our humanness, even at a young age we are desperate to escape our sin instead of facing it head-on. Because sin entered the world through one man (Rom. 5:12) we cannot escape it, and because God is holy and has intrinsically made us in His image and for His glory (Gen. 1:27; Isa. 43:7), we find ourselves caught in the great divide: separated and running from the judgment of the very One who created us.

We Compare

If we're not full-on hiding from our sin, we often attempt another act of self-preservation in our depraved state: the ever-popular art of comparison. If you've ever parented siblings, you've surely experienced this ultrapredictable phenomenon: if one kid is caught stealing a cookie, he'll point out that his brother stole two. As a teenager who happened to miss my curfew a time or two, my immediate defense (in my mind even if I didn't say it out loud) was something like, "Oh my word, I'm ten minutes late. If you only knew what other kids my age are out doing on the weekends." We find temporary comfort in pointing out those who appear to be worse sinners than we are, as if that negates our guilty state or somehow justifies our behavior.

I find it so telling that when Adam and Eve were asked to give an account for eating from the forbidden tree, without hesitation they both turned to blame-shifting: "The man said, 'The woman whom you gave to be with me, she gave me fruit of the tree, and I ate.' Then the LORD God said to the woman, 'What is this that you have done?' The woman said, 'The serpent deceived me, and I ate'" (Gen. 3:12–13). And the cover-up continues with us, becoming more and more complex and twisted as we try to front a superiority status that we'll never be able to maintain on our own strength, no matter how hard we try.

We Contribute

If we're not concealing or comparing our sin, we're often attempting to cover up the bad with a dose of our own good works. Many reason that in the short term it feels better to do something (then take credit for it), so we replace repentance with works, hoping our own contributions will somehow find favor with God and save us. But the Bible is clear that none of our human contributions will ever take care of the sin problem that resides deep within us (Eph. 2:8–9). Try spilling a gallon of milk on your carpet, then instead of calling the carpet guy and having it properly deep-cleaned, you cover the mess with a gorgeous new rug and call it a day. Problem solved, right? Far from it. Give it a few days, and the stench from that spoiled milk will eventually take over your entire house, not only damaging beyond repair your carpet and the fancy new rug covering it, but also seriously eating away at your pride and quality of life. So our sin remains in all of its foulness, penetrating deep down into the very fibers of our being, firmly taking up residence and wreaking havoc underneath the external beauty we've put on display.

John Piper explained it this way: "The question…is not, 'Can I do enough good works to outweigh my bad works?' No, the question is, 'Can I do one good work?' And the answer is no, which is why justification, our right standing with God, has to be not 99.99% grace and Christ, but 100%. And that is the way he saved us. By grace alone on the basis of Christ alone through faith alone to the glory of God's infinite, beautiful, superior worth alone."[1]

No matter what our cover-up method of choice is, a sobering truth remains: "Unless you repent, you too will all perish" (Luke 13:5 NIV).

The Dead-End Pursuit

I would not consider myself someone easily persuaded into following the crowd, but I have to admit that the temptation got the better of me on a recent road construction detour through my small Indiana town. The main roads had been blocked by the inconvenient barricades, and a new route had been clearly laid out in orange detour signs. The dilemma was, no one was following the newly marked path; instead, a large caravan of vehicles were all headed down a certain side road in an effort to get around the construction area more quickly. Everyone was doing it. It seemed to make sense. I was in a hurry to get out of that mess. Surely that many people knew what they were doing. Thirty minutes later, I found myself at the finish of a crowded dead-end street, carefully trying to maneuver my minivan around the army of vehicles that had gullibly found themselves in the same "stuck" situation as me. Instead of saving time by trying this "creative" alternative route, I was now highly frustrated, seriously late to my destination, and in a much bigger mess than when I started. With all that time now wasted, I'd have to start back at the beginning and take the official detoured route that I should have followed in the first place. It turned out that the authorities in charge of the construction project had provided the one and only path that would lead to freedom.

This world is known for its substitutes, dead ends, and empty pursuits when it comes to pursuing freedom from our sin. Ignoring the truth from Scripture that clearly points to the path that leads to life (Matt. 7:14),

1 John Piper. *"Can My Good Works Outweigh my Bad?"* Desiringgod.org. Desiring God Ministries. Web. 29 June 2016.

society is never lacking a misguided popular crowd to follow, a costly possession that returns void in its promise of delivering happiness, or a multitude of the latest self-proclaimed, quick-fix, self-help strategies that have taken over our newsfeeds that only result in disappointment time after time. These alternative routes almost always start out looking like they have great potential, but they never produce the results they claim.

The way of forgiveness can never be found in detours, distractions, or by disguising our sin. There is only one way to freedom, and His name is Jesus:

> The next day John saw Jesus coming toward him and said, "Look, the Lamb of God, who takes away the sin of the world!" (John 1:29)

The Only Way

I knew that I would be found out eventually. My cheeks felt flushed, not just from the warm air that had accumulated beneath the blankets, but from the uneasiness that was building deep down in my soul. No amount of stillness or shallow breathing, pretending, or avoidance could mask the truth that resided in that bright yellow butterfly room that day. I deserved what I had coming. I could hide for a while, but the fight to stay hidden was more than my broken heart could bear.

I hid because I was embarrassed.

I hid because I was broken.

I hid because I was afraid.

I hid because I expected the wrath that I deserved, instead of the grace that I received.

Adam and Eve hid because they were guilty before a holy God, and they knew it. God had already warned that the consequence for their disobedience was death (Gen. 3:3), and they were embarrassed, broken, and afraid, caught in their sin with no way out.

But God…two of the most powerful words ever spoken.

Author and theologian John MacArthur described it this way:

But God came seeking the hiding sinner. And here we find the first sight of grace, the first expression of kindness, the first indication that there might be a possibility for reconciliation because we don't find God thundering into the garden. We don't find a bolt of lightning coming out of heaven and incinerating Adam and Eve. Rather verse 9 (Genesis 3) says this, "Then the LORD God called to the man and said to him, 'Where are you?'" [2]

Grace. Sweet, unmerited favor from God that offers forgiveness, not because of who we are, but because of what Jesus has done. Grace. God's love in action, when forgiveness seems far away, and it is the last thing we deserve.

Grace shifts the focus off of us and onto Jesus. No amount of cover-up will take care of our sin. We can't conceal or compare our depraved state to someone else's, and we can't contribute any amount of good works that will act as sufficient payment. Our tireless pursuit of worldly detours will keep frustrating and getting us nowhere fast, only reinforcing the longing in our souls that remains unless a Savior steps in. We can't achieve forgiveness on our own. Not then. Not now. Not ever.

That's why Jesus came.

I'm not sure how long I stayed underneath those covers, but it was long enough that I had time to think through every possible scenario of how the whole ordeal would end. What would I say in my defense? How would my parents respond? I expected the worst but was met with gentleness and open arms. I hesitated to give affection but was embraced with unconditional love. I anticipated separation, rejection, and heavy consequences but was welcomed as a child who needed a place of forgiveness, comfort, and rest.

How much more is the Father's perfect love for us? God's grace doesn't come from a far-off place or from an unreachable Savior. It's not wavering or marred by human imperfection. Oh no. Because of Jesus, this grace comes from an accessible God, a compassionate Father whose heart is tuned in to hearing us whisper His name and is ready to welcome us with open arms. The indelible gift of grace bridges the gap that once separated

2 John MacArthur. *"Confrontation in Eden."* gty.org. Grace to You Ministries. Web. 29 June 2016.

us from God and is now a place in which we can continuously live…and can confidently stand (Rom. 5:1–2). The beautiful words of Isaiah speak of the merciful God who bestowed this kind of grace on the Israelites, and on us:

> Remember these things, O Jacob, and Israel, for you are my servant; I formed you; you are my servant; O Israel, you will not be forgotten by me. I have blotted out your transgressions like a cloud and your sins like mist; return to me, for I have redeemed you. Sing, O heavens, for the LORD has done it; shout, O depths of the earth; break forth into singing, O mountains, O forest, and every tree in it! For the LORD has redeemed Jacob, and will be glorified in Israel. (Isa. 44:21–23)

When it comes to our sin, crawling out from "underneath the covers" is an intimidating task. It takes losing our pride, humbling ourselves, admitting our need for a Savior, and turning the opposite direction from our selfish, rebellious ways. But when we finally do? We're met with the unmatched love of our Savior, who is longing to forgive and offer us freedom and an unspeakable joy like nothing we've ever known: "If my people, who are called by my name, will humble themselves and pray and seek my face and turn from their wicked ways, then I will hear from heaven, and I will forgive their sin and will heal their land" (2 Chron. 7:14 NIV).

Are you weary from the weight of your sin? Exhausted from all of the concealing, running, and pretending like you have it all together? Frustrated by your inability to beat this thing on your own? There's a better way. There is just one way. I invite you to run to Jesus and find the Way to forgiveness.

> "But the great thing to remember is that, though our feelings come and go, His love for us does not. It is not wearied by our sins, or our indifference; and, therefore, it is quite relentless in its determination that we shall be cured of those sins, at whatever cost to us, at whatever cost to Him." [3]

---

3 C. S. Lewis, *Mere Christianity.* 1952. HarperCollins Publishers.

PRAYER

Heavenly Father, thank You for Jesus, the Lamb of God, who takes away the sin of the world. In Him, we have redemption through His blood, the forgiveness of our trespasses, according to the riches of His grace. May the reality of Jesus' sacrifice humble us, and as we surrender our lives afresh to Him today, may your Holy Spirit empower us to pursue righteousness and godliness in ever increasing measure. In Jesus' name. Amen.

ELIZABETH'S TESTIMONY

I was born and raised in a Christian home by wonderful godly parents. I went to church every Sunday and was saved at the tender age of five on our way home from church. I was filled with such joy, awe, and love for Jesus that I had to share it! As soon as I got home, I promptly called every family member I knew.

As a baby Christian, I didn't know I was supposed to continue striving to be close to God. I learned all my Bible verses and prayed to confess my sins, but I had questions about the necessity of these practices. Questions tumbled around in my head. Soon I formed thoughts about God and being a Christian that were far from the truth. I felt that I had been saved, so I must be fine. I began viewing God as a stern, rules-only God. I did not see Him as the loving, caring, tender Father He is. I feared asking questions, believing I should have had it all figured out.

I entered what I like to call my "prodigal daughter" phase. I was sixteen when my granny, whom I was extremely close to, passed away suddenly. I tried to be strong for my grieving parents but was struggling with depression and thoughts of harming myself. Thankfully, God was working, even though I was running from Him. He reminded me that my parents needed me, and it was that awareness that kept me from hurting myself.

At the age of seventeen, I got my first real job and was letting the people I worked with influence me. Yes, you truly are whom you hang out with. I started to date my first real boyfriend. Growing up, I was the awkward late bloomer. All of my friends were prettier and curvier, and that did not go unnoticed by the boys. Now it was my turn! I felt powerful knowing I could turn heads with my looks. Within one year, that relationship ended, and God brought my now husband, Cole, into my life.

We decided we loved each other enough to have sex. I wish I could say I was only intimate with him, but I made some meaningless choices that caused us to go separate ways. He was the one I loved. He is solid and loving and my family adored him. But I ended up cheating on him with several others because I loved the high I got from knowing that someone else thought I was beautiful.

I didn't realize that most of them only wanted what I could give them sexually. Mostly I didn't care, but deep down I knew it was wrong and God was not happy. I was living a double life at home and at church. I would lie to my parents, go to parties, and be in places where I shouldn't have been. I was uncomfortable at church but put on a front.

At nineteen, things started to change. Cole and I briefly began dating again before he moved back to his hometown. We continued a long-distance relationship, but it was rocky. I continued my free-love ways but started to notice it wasn't all fun and games anymore. At the end of the year, Cole asked me to join him. A few months later, I packed up all my things, said a tearful good-bye to family and friends, and ran away from my mistakes.

Guilt follows. After moving, I didn't start going to church for quite some time. When I finally went to church, I was brought to tears over my many sins. Slowly I began to be convicted about my need to ask Cole to forgive me for all those times I had been unfaithful to him. I assumed it would be the end of our relationship, but he loved and forgave me. At the end of the year, Cole asked me to marry him. We married the following June.

I joined a Bible study at church and soon realized God wanted the real me, not the person I was pretending to be. Two years into our marriage, when a sweet little angel was born into our lives, I realized my need for my Savior.

This prodigal daughter came limping back to her loving Father. He opened His arms wide to me and said, "Welcome home. I've missed you!"

I still struggle with forgiving myself for the choices I made, but I am grateful they led me back to God.

As I studied the Bible I learned of God's great love for me. When I read the story about how God forgave a prostitute, I felt He was talking to me. I am a living testimony of God's amazing forgiveness, mercy, grace, and unconditional love. I'm not perfect, but God doesn't require that of me. He set me free! I am forgiven and redeemed!

- - - - - - - - - -

His divine power has granted to us all things that pertain to life and godliness.
through the knowledge of Him who called us to his own glory and excellence.

(2 Peter 1:3)

Monday

READ: Ephesians 1:3-7
SOAP: Ephesians 1:7

Scripture - Write out the **Scripture** passage for the day.

Observations - Write down 1 or 2 **observations** from the passage.

Applications - Write down 1 or 2 **applications** from the passage.

Pray - Write out a **prayer** over what you learned from today's passage.

-Visit our website today for the corresponding blog post!-

Tuesday

READ: John 3:16-21
SOAP: John 3:16

Scripture - Write out the **Scripture** passage for the day.

Observations - Write down 1 or 2 **observations** from the passage.

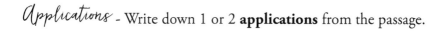

Applications - Write down 1 or 2 **applications** from the passage.

Pray - Write out a **prayer** over what you learned from today's passage.

Wednesday

READ: Luke 13:1-5
SOAP: Luke 13:5

Scripture - Write out the **Scripture** passage for the day.

Observations - Write down 1 or 2 **observations** from the passage.

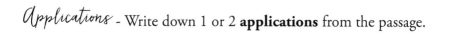

Wednesday

Applications - Write down 1 or 2 **applications** from the passage.

Pray - Write out a **prayer** over what you learned from today's passage.

-Visit our website today for the corresponding blog post!-

Thursday

READ: John 1:26-30
SOAP: John 1:29

Scripture - Write out the **Scripture** passage for the day.

Observations - Write down 1 or 2 **observations** from the passage.

Thursday

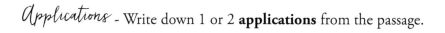

Applications - Write down 1 or 2 **applications** from the passage.

Pray - Write out a **prayer** over what you learned from today's passage.

Friday

READ: 2 Chronicles 7:12-16
SOAP: 2 Chronicles 7:14

Scripture - Write out the **Scripture** passage for the day.

Observations - Write down 1 or 2 **observations** from the passage.

Friday

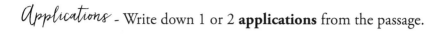

Applications - Write down 1 or 2 **applications** from the passage.

Pray - Write out a **prayer** over what you learned from today's passage.

-Visit our website today for the corresponding blog post!-

Reflection Questions

1. What unhealthy actions or attitudes about your sin do you continue to pursue, despite the fact that they lead to the same undesirable consequences?

2. What is your first response when someone holds you accountable for your sin?

3. Are you quick to confess your sins to Jesus, or do you try to justify or excuse them?

4. Understanding there is no sin too great for Jesus to forgive, lay a yet-unconfessed sin at the feet of Jesus, believing He has the power and the desire to forgive you.

5. How does experiencing God's grace give hope and purpose to your future?

My Response

Week 3

Week 3 Challenge (Note: You can find this listed in our Monday blog post):

Prayer focus for this week: Spend time praying for your friends.

Praying	Praise
Monday	
Tuesday	
Wednesday	
Thursday	
Friday	

"As far as the east is from the west, so far does he remove our transgressions from us".

PSALM 103:12

Scripture for Week 3

MONDAY   *1 JOHN 1:5-9 (ESV)*

⁵ This is the message we have heard from him and proclaim to you, that God is light, and in him is no darkness at all. ⁶ If we say we have fellowship with him while we walk in darkness, we lie and do not practice the truth. ⁷ But if we walk in the light, as he is in the light, we have fellowship with one another, and the blood of Jesus his Son cleanses us from all sin. ⁸ If we say we have no sin, we deceive ourselves, and the truth is not in us. ⁹ If we confess our sins, he is faithful and just to forgive us our sins and to cleanse us from all unrighteousness.

TUESDAY   *MICAH 7:18-19 (ESV)*

¹⁸ Who is a God like you, pardoning iniquity

and passing over transgression

for the remnant of his inheritance?

He does not retain his anger forever,

because he delights in steadfast love.

¹⁹ He will again have compassion on us;

he will tread our iniquities underfoot.

You will cast all our sins

into the depths of the sea.

WEDNESDAY   *HEBREWS 9:23-28 (ESV)*

²³ Thus it was necessary for the copies of the heavenly things to be purified with these rites, but the heavenly things themselves with better sacrifices than these. ²⁴ For Christ has entered, not into holy places made with hands, which are copies of the true things, but into heaven itself, now to appear in the presence of God on our behalf. ²⁵ Nor was it to offer himself repeatedly, as the high priest

enters the holy places every year with blood not his own, ²⁶ for then he would have had to suffer repeatedly since the foundation of the world. But as it is, he has appeared once for all at the end of the ages to put away sin by the sacrifice of himself.²⁷ And just as it is appointed for man to die once, and after that comes judgment, ²⁸ so Christ, having been offered once to bear the sins of many, will appear a second time, not to deal with sin but to save those who are eagerly waiting for him. **THURSDAY** *PSALM ¹⁰³:¹¹-¹³ (ESV)*

¹¹ For as high as the heavens are above the earth,

    so great is his steadfast love toward those who fear him;

¹² as far as the east is from the west,

    so far does he remove our transgressions from us.

¹³ As a father shows compassion to his children,

    so the Lord shows compassion to those who fear him.

FRIDAY   *ISAIAH 38:17-19 (ESV)*

¹⁷ Behold, it was for my welfare

    that I had great bitterness;

but in love you have delivered my life

    from the pit of destruction,

for you have cast all my sins

    behind your back.

¹⁸ For Sheol does not thank you;

    death does not praise you;

those who go down to the pit do not hope

    for your faithfulness.

¹⁹ The living, the living, he thanks you,

    as I do this day;

the father makes known to the children

    your faithfulness.

3

THE DEPTH OF OUR FORGIVENESS

BY JEN THORN

How deep the father's love for us.
How vast beyond all measure.
That He should give His only Son
To make a wretch His treasure.[1]

I LOVE SINGING these words by Stuart Townend. Out of this profound love comes God's deep forgiveness. It is so deep, in fact, that we don't have an adequate way of describing it. The Bible gives us a number of different word pictures to help us understand and reflect on this life-changing truth. God's Word says our sins have been removed from us as far as the east is from the west (Ps. 103:12), and they've been thrown into the deepest part of the ocean, and God has stomped them into the ground (Mic. 7:19). But even this can't fully express the depths of God's forgiveness.

Isaiah 59:1–2 tells us that sin has separated mankind from God. Sin is the destroyer of all things. It has ruined creation; it has brought sickness, disease, every kind of imaginable evil, and ultimately death. This horrific monster has also brought separation and disharmony among man and animals, man and man, and most devastatingly, between man and God.

---

1 Stuart Townend, *"How Deep the Father's Love for Us"* Copyright © 1995 Thankyou Music (Adm. by CapitolCMGPublishing.com excl. UK & Europe, adm. by Integrity Music, part of the David C Cook family, songs@integritymusic.com)

Seeing that sin's corruption reaches into the furthest corners of our hearts, we are helpless and in desperate need of a Savior. God knew this, and in His infinite mercy and grace He sent His Son to die in order to pay sin's ransom, bridge the gap, and set us free.

Forgiveness is God's pardoning of sinners through the sacrifice of His Son.

But how deep does the forgiveness of God toward His people go? Is there a limit to His mercy? Is there a breaking point to His love? Does the power of Christ's blood end someplace?

Thankfully, "He does not treat us as our sins deserve or repay us according to our iniquities" (Ps. 103:10 NIV).

God's Forgiveness Makes Us His Friends

> "The Scripture was fulfilled that says, "Abraham believed God, and it was counted to him as righteousness"— and he was called a friend of God" (James 2:23).

Those who have not placed their trust in Jesus have God as their Judge (Ps. 7:11–12). This is frightening because sin makes them guilty of death (Rom. 6:23) and deserving of God's just anger. The punishment of sin is fair and just.

Those who are condemned cannot enjoy an intimate relationship with God, for no one can stand before God and His just wrath and survive. We were once people like this. Separation and death were what we deserved.

But God. This beautiful phrase is seen a number of times in the Scriptures, and it is a phrase of hope (italics mine):

> You meant evil against me; *but God* meant it for good, in order to. . .save many people alive. (Gen. 50:20 NKJV)

> My flesh and my heart may fail; *but God* is the strength of my heart and my portion forever. (Ps. 73:26)

> Their beauty shall be consumed in the grave... *But God* will redeem

my soul from the power of the grave. (Ps. 49:14–15 NKJV)

For scarcely for a righteous man will one die; yet perhaps for a good man someone would even dare to die. But God demonstrates His own love toward us, in that while we were still sinners, Christ died for us. (Rom. 5:7–8 NKJV)

While we were sinners and were sinning, Christ died for us. This is beautiful, uplifting hope. Because while God is still the judge, He has now also become our Savior and our Advocate, our Redeemer! "The LORD is our judge; the LORD is our lawgiver; the LORD is our king; he will save us" (Is. 33:22).

Because of Jesus' sacrifice we are no longer condemned. Instead, we have peace with God and a relationship that is eternally secure. Nothing and no one can snatch us away and undo the precious payment of Christ's atoning blood. This changes everything, for now this Judge becomes our Father, and our enemy (Rom. 5:10) becomes our Friend.

I love hanging out with my friends, sharing stories, sipping coffee, encouraging each other through words of truth, or bumming around a store. Friendship is important. It brings much joy and laughter into our lives. But friendship has its limits. There are no perfect friends, and I highly doubt that any friend of mine, no matter how close we are, would go to jail for me or pay for my crimes.

But this doesn't mean a friend like that does not exist. While Jesus was on earth He became known as the "friend of sinners." As a matter of fact, the Pharisees were annoyed with Him for hanging out with disreputable people: "The Son of Man has come eating and drinking, and you say, 'Look at him! A glutton and a drunkard, a friend of tax collectors and sinners!'" (Luke 7:34)

The religious leaders believed that Jesus was defiling Himself by being in the same room with tax collectors, common fishermen, prostitutes, and other lowlifes. In their minds, Jesus had no business having anything to do with that kind. The Pharisees had an obsession with religious purity, and that meant they went through great lengths to avoid sinners. What Jesus was doing was unthinkable.

But Jesus was doing more than socializing. Jesus didn't come to simply hang out and have a good time. He truly cared for those people. He had real affection for them. Jesus knew the condition of their hearts, their helplessness, and what they needed in order to find life that went beyond this world. Those sinners, as all sinners do, needed a friend who spoke the truth and showed them the truth. Jesus was this truth, a friend who was willing to lay His life down so they could be saved. As He said, "Greater love has no one than this, that someone lay down his life for his friends" (John 15:13).

In Jesus we have a friend who is willing to experience death and the wrath of God for us. Jesus didn't just talk about being willing to lay down His life. He actually did lay it down, willingly. As our Friend He takes interest in things that bring joy to us, and He cares when we are hurting.

Doesn't this humble you? It humbles me, because I am not a great friend to Jesus. All too often I am a fair-weather friend. Have you ever felt this way? We stick around when things are going in our favor, but as soon as things get a little rough we complain, throw up our fists, and look for help elsewhere. We act like He is our BFF when the sun is shining and we are feeling blessed, but when hard times hit or prayers seem to go unanswered, we give Him the cold shoulder.

Sometimes we think we know better than God does. We read His Word and feel uncomfortable or offended at what He says, and so we choose to not believe it or to twist His words into a theology that makes us feel better, all the while forgetting that God's ways are not our ways and that we must trust that He knows better.

Other times we are plain forgetful. We forget all that Jesus did and does for us. We forget how He lived so we could receive His righteousness. We forget how He suffered so we could be forgiven. And we forget the sheer power of His resurrection that grants us power and victory over sin. We forget that His greatness cannot be compared with anything on this earth and that one day He will come again and we will see Him in His full glory and power.

The forgiveness we have in Jesus covers our forgetfulness and our fickle love toward our divine friend, but it also makes having a friendship with Christ possible.

God's Forgiveness Makes Him Our Father

Father's Day for many can be a difficult day. For some, the pain of loss makes Father's Day hard to celebrate. I know this well as my dad passed away when I was seventeen. Others had or have fathers who were not very present, not very loving, not very kind, and possibly even abusive. So for some, seeing God as Father is difficult to imagine, because all they have are painful memories of the failures of their own dad.

My heart breaks for you if you are in this situation, but remember that God is not like man. He will not leave you; He will not be unkind to you; He will not abuse you. His character makes these failures impossible. But He can and does love you with an overwhelming fatherly love. God's love is one that is willing to forgive people who sin against Him daily, through the death of His Son, Jesus Christ, and to adopt them into His family as His own. No longer are we enemies or strangers; we are now a child of the Great High King.

As our perfect heavenly Father, He hears you when you pray. God listens intently to the prayers of His children, whether they are exclamations of praise, cries of help, words of joy and excitement, or prayers of sorrow. He hears every word you say to Him because He has promised He would never leave you (Deut. 31:6). God, your Father, cares tremendously for those who were purchased by the precious blood of His Son!

How deep is the forgiveness and love of God toward us? So deep that He is willing to make sinful people, like you and me, His children. He becomes our perfect Father. And as Father, He protects the souls of His children, He provides them with all they need for life and godliness (2 Peter 1:3), He teaches them His ways, He has an inheritance for them that is unimaginable, and He is preparing a home for them where nothing can harm them or separate them from Himself again. This is only possible because of the forgiveness we have in Jesus.

God's Forgiveness Makes Us Pure

The forgiveness we have doesn't just affect our relational standing with God. It also affects our person. Sin is so filthy. It stains everything with a dirt that cannot be removed.

This reminds me of a fairy tale I heard as a child. It's about two sisters. Through a series of events, one of the sisters gets lost and finds herself at the house of an old woman. She stays with her, shaking out her blankets, fluffing her pillows, and doing other chores. When it is time for her to go home, she passes under a gate and is rewarded with gold poured out on her. When she arrives back home, the second sister sees all this gold and she also wants to receive this reward, so she goes through the same series of events and ends up at the old woman's house. But this girl complains all the time and is terribly lazy. She does as little work as possible, waiting for the times that she can finally go home. When it is time for her to return to her family she passes under the same gate, but instead of being rewarded with gold, tar pours out all over her, and for the rest of her life this tar sticks to her.

Sin is like that tar. It sticks to us, and no matter what we try to do we are helpless to remove it. But through the forgiveness we have in Jesus, the sticky stain of sin is washed away, and we are made pure. Pure! This means that when God looks at us He sees us without a single blemish. He takes Christ's work of righteousness and covers us, just like the gold that covered the first sister. It cannot be removed; it cannot be stolen or lost.

In Psalm 51:7 we get another picture of what the righteousness of Christ is like. David wrote that we are washed whiter than snow. That is impossible for me to imagine. What could be whiter than snow? Those who trust in Jesus, that's who, and this means you!

The question we have to ask then is, how does God do it? Does He simply forget our sins (Heb. 8:12)? He tells us, "I, even I, am he who blots out your transgressions, for my own sake, and remembers your sins no more" (Isa. 43:25 NIV).

When someone sins against me and says they are truly sorry, I have no problem forgiving them, but I still remember. And sometimes this remembering can lead to old wounds reopening. Remembering the wrong that someone has done against us can tempt us to become bitter or a little resentful. It can bring back that sick feeling in the pit of your stomach or the anger in your heart, and we must fight against that.

Can God forget anything? No. God does not literally forget our sin. He can't, because He is omniscient; He knows all things (Ps. 139). This is a part of what makes Him God. Scripture says, "Nothing in all creation is hidden from God's sight. Everything is uncovered and laid bare before the eyes of him to whom we must give account" (Heb. 4:13 NIV).

So what does it mean when Isaiah says that God does not remember our sins? Here we see the largeness of God's heart as well as His infinite love. When God forgives, He no longer holds our sins against us. Here is the awesomeness of God; He knows exactly what we have done to Him and to others, and yet He does not hang it over us. He does not feel bitterness, anger, or resentment toward us. When God forgives us, it is as if He has forgotten all about it.

Are you beginning to see the depth of God's forgiveness?

Nineteenth-century theologian Charles Spurgeon said, "Can you appropriate that thought? From the crown of your head to the sole of your foot, God is examining you now; his scalpel is in your heart, his lancet in your breast. He is searching your heart and trying your reins; he knows you behind and before. 'Thou God seest me; thou seest me entirely.'"[2]

The fact that He knows everything there is to know, including everything there is to know about us, and doesn't forget, but instead loves and blesses us should bring us to tears. Tears of gratitude, awe, love, and joy.

God's Forgiveness Cleanses Our Consciences

We all have a conscience. It is that voice inside you that tells you if something you are doing is right or wrong. Our conscience, like the rest of us, is broken on account of sin. It works, but it is no longer perfectly accurate. Sometimes our conscience is too sensitive, and at other times it has become hardened to the sins we commit.

Some of us are plagued by our conscience regarding our past sins, and some of us have a conscience that is constantly reminding us how drastically we fall short of God's perfection on a daily basis. Satan uses this against us often. He takes that knife of a guilty conscience and pushes it even deeper into our soul. He wants us to despair, to make us believe all is hopeless. Satan uses our broken conscience to steer us away from God. He tries to make us feel guilty about things we don't need to feel guilty about anymore, and he tries to numb our conscience to things that actually are

2 Charles H. Spurgeon. Sermon entitled "*Omniscience*," June 15, 1856. Romans45.org. Web. 29 June 2016.

sin. We need our conscience cleansed and corrected.

The forgiveness that Christ offers goes so deep that it cleans the depth of our being. It reaches all the way to our conscience. "How much more, then, will the blood of Christ, who through the eternal Spirit offered himself unblemished to God, cleanse our consciences from acts that lead to death, so that we may serve the living God!" (Heb. 9:14 NIV)

No longer do we need to agonize over the guilt that wants to plague us because of our shortcomings and the sins we have committed against others and against God.

In Worms, Germany, in 1521, Martin Luther was tried for heresy. The more Martin Luther had studied his Bible the more he began to see the errors that were being taught in the Catholic church. In his response to these errors he wrote ninety-five theses airing his concerns and nailed them to the church door in Wittenberg. Bedlam broke out within the church and Martin was arrested. He was given the chance to recant, but his response was, "My conscience is held captive to the word of God." And the Protestant church was born.[3]

The forgiveness we have in Jesus makes this possible because it reaches the depths of our conscience. It allows us to be able to have a conscience that works better, one that can see the difference between truth and error. Forgiveness can set us free from a guilty conscience and give us a conscience that is "held captive to the word of God."

The depth of God's forgiveness is far deeper than we realize. We cannot reach the bottom of it, but we are invited to swim in it. These are deep but safe waters. Like the fish of the sea, whose lives are only possible in the waters gathered by the creative power of our God, we, too, live in the waters of forgiveness. These waters have no boundaries, no floor, and no danger.

Late author Jerry Bridges said it well when he wrote, "Our sins have been put away. To use the language of the Scriptures…they are completely removed, put behind God's back, blotted out, remembered no more, and hurled into the depths of the sea."[4]

---

3 Luther, Martin. *"Reply to the Diet of Worms, April 18, 1521."* Luther's Works, 33: Career of the Reformer III. Saint Louis, MO: Concordia House, 1955
4 Bridges, Jerry, *"The Gospel For Real Life"*, 2002

PRAYER

Heavenly Father, thank You for Your steadfast love. The Savior's blood has paid sin's ransom and set us free. We need not fear losing Your love or having You turn your back on us when we disappoint You. You hear our every cry and are attentive to our every need. In Your omniscience, You meet our needs before we are even aware of them, and You care for us as only a loving, omnipotent Father could do. You, oh Lord, are our Rock and Redeemer. Father, we love and adore You. In Jesus' name. Amen.

JESSICA'S TESTIMONY

Forgiveness, such a beautiful word. In my story, I've had to forgive myself, forgive others, and have had to ask others to forgive me. I was given up for adoption when I was an infant. At sixteen days old, a beautiful, giving lady named Judy and her husband traveled two hours on a hot September day, in a car with no air conditioning, to pick up a tiny little girl and give her a family.

I never felt different or as if I didn't belong in my family. My mom is the best possible mother I could have ever wished for. She and I have always said that we are so grateful that God put us together. I was raised with one sister (Mom's biological daughter), a brother (adopted like me) and two step-brothers. From the beginning, Mom loved each of us as if we were all her biological children; she made no distinction among us.

When I began my search for my biological mother, it wasn't from a desire to find my "real" mom, nor was it to fill any missing piece in my life. I already had a family, so it wasn't as if I was missing anything. My search for my biological mother was purely out of a need for more medical information and curiosity about my heritage.

I was stationed in Japan when my search really began. When I joined the US Navy I had a note put into my adoption record that if any medical history came in I would like to be notified. In March 1994 that letter came, a letter from the adoption agency stating that my biological mother had contacted them with more medical information. It stated that she had cancer, and I had a half sister who had a heart condition. There was nothing more specific than that, and the records would need to be opened in order for me to learn more.

My mom called me to let me know about the letter and asked me what I wanted to do. Of course I wanted to know more, so my mom filed the paperwork to petition the courts to have the records opened for more information. About two months later another letter arrived at home and I received a 2:00 a.m. call in Japan from my sister telling me the specifics of my adoption. Unbeknownst to me, my mom had searched for my biological mother's phone number, gathered all the information about her, and gave the information to my sister before she called me.

Over the next twelve hours, I made two calls to my biological mother's house. We were eventually able to talk on the phone, and our conversation lasted well over one hour. She told me a little about my heritage, what kind of cancer she had, and the nature of my half sister's heart condition. I learned I had a half brother too, and we discussed meeting during the summer and we exchanged mailing addresses.

When I came home on leave that summer, I made plans to meet my biological mother. She lived about a five-hour drive away from my home. I told my mom that I couldn't go if she didn't want to go with me. I can't imagine the love it took for Mom to go with me. She was very nervous about going, but she supported me 100 percent and went with me anyway. I know now that was hard for her, but at the time I selfishly knew I couldn't go if she wasn't with me.

The meeting with my biological mother went well. She wouldn't tell me who my biological father is, and that's been a thorn in our relationship ever since. We kept in touch for a few years, but the sticking point in our relationship has always been the identity of my biological father. It has become such an issue with us that I no longer have a relationship with her or my half sister. I do have a relationship with my biological half brother, but as I don't want to cause problems for him with his mother, I tread lightly and stay a bit in the distance.

Through all of this, my mom and sister stood by me and supported me fully. I never considered how difficult it was for my mom to go through that entire process with me. I never considered that my mom, my sweet mom, would be hurt through the experience. Although she would never say it, it was difficult for her to see me meeting my biological mother. I also never considered that my sister would wonder if she might be replaced by my biological half sister. In my mind, she is my sister, the one I prayed for when my mom was pregnant. Additionally, I already had three brothers, so I didn't want another brother either. In the end, I hurt my mom and sister, two people I would never have ever wanted to hurt or meant to hurt.

I have apologized to my mom and sister and asked them to forgive me. Of course, being the beautiful ladies that they are, they've both told me there was nothing to forgive. Although Mom told me she understands my desire to know more information about where I came from and my medical history, I've had to forgive myself for being insensitive to their feelings during that time.

I have no relationship with my biological mother and half sister and believe the issue of the identity of my biological father has made it difficult for us to move forward. I will always have a deep respect for my biological mother for giving me up. Her unselfish act allowed me the chance for a better life. I have forgiven her for her unwillingness to tell me who my biological father is, even though I believe I have a right to know that piece of my history. I've accepted the fact that I likely will never know.

I know all of this would not have been possible if I didn't have a mother who loves the Lord. She taught her two daughters the meaning of loving God, forgiveness, to value family, and the meaning of unconditional love. I thank God for my mom and my sister. They are two beautiful, loving, forgiving women with amazing hearts. I am so thankful that God put the three of us together; I am so thankful for my family.

- - - - - - - - - -

Yet you are he who took me from the womb;
you made me trust you at my mother's breasts.

(Ps. 22:9)

Monday

READ: 1 John 1:5-9
SOAP: 1 John 1:9

Scripture - Write out the **Scripture** passage for the day.

Observations - Write down 1 or 2 **observations** from the passage.

Monday

Applications - Write down 1 or 2 **applications** from the passage.

Pray - Write out a **prayer** over what you learned from today's passage.

-Visit our website today for the corresponding blog post!-

Tuesday

READ: Micah 7:18-19
SOAP: Micah 7:19

Scripture - Write out the **Scripture** passage for the day.

Observations - Write down 1 or 2 **observations** from the passage.

Tuesday

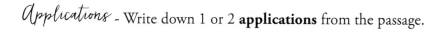

Applications - Write down 1 or 2 **applications** from the passage.

Pray - Write out a **prayer** over what you learned from today's passage.

Wednesday

READ: Hebrews 9:23-28
SOAP: Hebrews 9:28

Scripture - Write out the **Scripture** passage for the day.

Observations - Write down 1 or 2 **observations** from the passage.

Wednesday

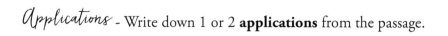 - Write down 1 or 2 **applications** from the passage.

Pray - Write out a **prayer** over what you learned from today's passage.

-Visit our website today for the corresponding blog post!-

Thursday

READ: Psalm 103:11-13
SOAP: Psalm 103:12

Scripture - Write out the **Scripture** passage for the day.

Observations - Write down 1 or 2 **observations** from the passage.

Thursday

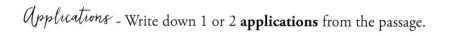

Applications - Write down 1 or 2 **applications** from the passage.

Pray - Write out a **prayer** over what you learned from today's passage.

Friday

READ: Isaiah 38:17-19
SOAP: Isaiah 38:17

Scripture - Write out the **Scripture** passage for the day.

Observations - Write down 1 or 2 **observations** from the passage.

Friday

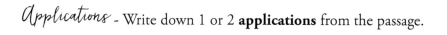

Applications - Write down 1 or 2 **applications** from the passage.

Pray - Write out a **prayer** over what you learned from today's passage.

-Visit our website today for the corresponding blog post!-

Reflection Questions

1. Think about what sin seems to trip you up the most. How does it make you feel that the infinite mercy and grace of Jesus continually covers those confessed sins? Thank Him today for His faithfulness to forgive you for those reoccurring sins.

2. Are there those in your life you need to forgive? What keeps you from forgiving them as God has forgiven you?

3. Have you accepted the deep love that God has for you? If you have a hard time accepting that love, pray and ask Him to allow your heart to openly accept His unconditional love.

4. Knowing that God understands everything about you, yet continues to love and bless you even when you are your worst self, what is your response to that depth of love?

5. Ask God to teach you how to keep "short account" with Him, that is, confessing your sins quickly and accepting the forgiveness He so graciously offers.

My Response

Week 4

Week 4 Challenge (Note: You can find this listed in our Monday blog post):

Prayer focus for this week: Spend time praying for your church.

Praying	Praise
Monday	
Tuesday	
Wednesday	
Thursday	
Friday	

"Therefore, if anyone is in Christ,
he is a new creation.
The old has passed away;
behold, the new has come".

2 CORINTHIANS 5:17

Scripture for Week 4

MONDAY 2 CORINTHIANS 5 (ESV)

For we know that if the tent that is our earthly home is destroyed, we have a building from God, a house not made with hands, eternal in the heavens. ² For in this tent we groan, longing to put on our heavenly dwelling, ³ if indeed by putting it on we may not be found naked. ⁴ For while we are still in this tent, we groan, being burdened—not that we would be unclothed, but that we would be further clothed, so that what is mortal may be swallowed up by life. ⁵ He who has prepared us for this very thing is God, who has given us the Spirit as a guarantee.

⁶ So we are always of good courage. We know that while we are at home in the body we are away from the Lord, ⁷ for we walk by faith, not by sight. ⁸ Yes, we are of good courage, and we would rather be away from the body and at home with the Lord. ⁹ So whether we are at home or away, we make it our aim to please him. ¹⁰ For we must all appear before the judgment seat of Christ, so that each one may receive what is due for what he has done in the body, whether good or evil.

¹¹ Therefore, knowing the fear of the Lord, we persuade others. But what we are is known to God, and I hope it is known also to your conscience. ¹² We are not commending ourselves to you again but giving you cause to boast about us, so that you may be able to answer those who boast about outward appearance and not about what is in the heart. ¹³ For if we are beside ourselves, it is for God; if we are in our right mind, it is for you. ¹⁴ For the love of Christ controls us, because we have concluded this: that one has died for all, therefore all have died;¹⁵ and he died for all, that those who live might no longer live for themselves but for him who for their sake died and was raised.

¹⁶ From now on, therefore, we regard no one according to the flesh. Even though we once regarded Christ according to the flesh, we regard him thus no longer. ¹⁷ Therefore, if anyone is in Christ,

88 WEEK 4   YOU ARE FORGIVEN

he is a new creation. The old has passed away; behold, the new has come. [18] All this is from God, who through Christ reconciled us to himself and gave us the ministry of reconciliation; [19] that is, in Christ God was reconciling the world to himself, not counting their trespasses against them, and entrusting to us the message of reconciliation. [20] Therefore, we are ambassadors for Christ, God making his appeal through us. We implore you on behalf of Christ, be reconciled to God. [21] For our sake he made him to be sin who knew no sin, so that in him we might become the righteousness of God.

TUESDAY   *ROMANS 12:1-2 (ESV)*

[12] I appeal to you therefore, brothers, by the mercies of God, to present your bodies as a living sacrifice, holy and acceptable to God, which is your spiritual worship. [2] Do not be conformed to this world, but be transformed by the renewal of your mind, that by testing you may discern what is the will of God, what is good and acceptable and perfect.

WEDNESDAY   *ROMANS 6:1-10 (ESV)*

[6] What shall we say then? Are we to continue in sin that grace may abound? [2] By no means! How can we who died to sin still live in it? [3] Do you not know that all of us who have been baptized into Christ Jesus were baptized into his death? [4] We were buried therefore with him by baptism into death, in order that, just as Christ was raised from the dead by the glory of the Father, we too might walk in newness of life.

[5] For if we have been united with him in a death like his, we shall certainly be united with him in a resurrection like his. [6] We know that our old self was crucified with him in order that the body of sin might be brought to nothing, so that we would no longer be enslaved to sin. [7] For one who has died has been set free from sin. [8] Now if we have died with Christ, we believe that we will also live with him. [9] We know that Christ, being raised from

the dead, will never die again; death no longer has dominion over him. [10] For the death he died he died to sin, once for all, but the life he lives he lives to God.

THURSDAY   *COLOSSIANS 3:1-17 (ESV)*

[3] If then you have been raised with Christ, seek the things that are above, where Christ is,seated at the right hand of God. [2] Set your minds on things that are above, not on things that are on earth. [3] For you have died, and your life is hidden with Christ in God. [4] When Christ who is your life appears, then you also will appear with him in glory.

[5] Put to death therefore what is earthly in you: sexual immorality, impurity, passion, evil desire, and covetousness, which is idolatry. [6] On account of these the wrath of God is coming. [7] In these you too once walked, when you were living in them. [8] But now you must put them all away: anger, wrath, malice, slander, and obscene talk from your mouth. [9] Do not lie to one another, seeing that you have put off the old self with its practices [10] and have put on the new self, which is being renewed in knowledge after the image of its creator. [11] Here there is not Greek and Jew, circumcised and uncircumcised, barbarian, Scythian, slave, free; but Christ is all, and in all.

[12] Put on then, as God's chosen ones, holy and beloved, compassionate hearts, kindness,humility, meekness, and patience, [13] bearing with one another and, if one has a complaint against another, forgiving each other; as the Lord has forgiven you, so you also must forgive.[14] And above all these put on love, which binds everything together in perfect harmony. [15] And let the peace of Christ rule in your hearts, to which indeed you were called in one body. And be thankful. [16] Let the word of Christ dwell in you richly, teaching and admonishing one another in all wisdom, singing psalms and hymns and spiritual songs, with thankfulness in your hearts to God. [17] And whatever you do, in word or deed, do everything in the name of the Lord Jesus,giving thanks to God the Father through him.

[5] Everyone who believes that Jesus is the Christ has been born of God, and everyone who loves the Father loves whoever has been born of him. [2] By this we know that we love the children of God, when we love God and obey his commandments. [3] For this is the love of God, that we keep his commandments. And his commandments are not burdensome. [4] For everyone who has been born of God overcomes the world. And this is the victory that has overcome the world—our faith.

4

THE RESULT OF FORGIVENESS

BY JOY FORNEY

Getting There

HAVE YOU BEEN enjoying our journey so far? Are you beginning to see how much the God of the universe loves you and cares about you? We're now heading into the result of forgiveness. We've gained an understanding of what forgiveness is, what it looks like, and how to truly receive it. Now we want to know what result it has in the outpouring of our life.

What are some of the results of forgiveness? Before you read on, take a moment to journal your thoughts. What would it look like in your life or in the life of someone else to truly understand, grasp, and live in the light of real forgiveness? Think about this for a moment. The results of forgiveness are many, but here are just a few:

- True freedom

- A deep love for yourself and others

- A lightness and a joy that go down deep into your soul and all the way to your toes

- Peace

Sounds good right? So how do we get there? How do we get from head knowledge to heart knowledge? From believing to living out in the every day? Let's use to really dive deep into understanding the transformation and results of being forgiven.

> "Therefore, having put away falsehood, let each one of you speak the truth with his neighbor, for we are members one of another. Be angry and do not sin; do not let the sun go down on your anger, and give no opportunity to the devil. Let the thief no longer steal, but rather let him labor, doing honest work with his own hands, so that he may have something to share with anyone in need. Let no corrupting talk come out of your mouths, but only such as is good for building up, as fits the occasion, that it may give grace to those who hear. And do not grieve the Holy Spirit of God, by whom you were sealed for the day of redemption. Let all bitterness and wrath and anger and clamor and slander be put away from you, along with all malice. Be kind to one another, tenderhearted, forgiving one another, as God in Christ forgave you." (Eph. 4:25–32)

Paul is explaining to us who we are and how we are to put on our new self. We are to put off lying and just speak the truth. We are to put off stealing and put on generosity; put away anger and bitterness and put on forgiveness. But here is the difference between Christianity and any other religion: Christianity doesn't mimic moral behavior. Islam does that. Confucianism does that. Buddhism does that. Every major religion tells you to forgive and be kind. Every one.

The difference here is that Paul is telling Christians to live into our identity. We are to live out of what is already granted in us and for us. He is telling us, not to live out good behavior, follow a set of rules, and go about your day and be a good person. No. He is telling us who we are in Christ and how we can live because of that.

Remind yourself of who you are now that God in Christ has forgiven you. That is the secret. That is the amazing truth that walks with you through the day. And don't grieve the Holy Spirit of God whom you received at the day of redemption. What Paul is telling you is that when you are angry or bitter or frustrated, you aren't supposed to say, "I've got to stop being bitter. Stop it. Really just stop." When you are lying don't tell yourself, "Don't lie. That is wrong. Christians don't act like that." Instead, look at Jesus Christ on the cross. Look at Him deeply, and come to the place where you say, "How can I ever repay someone who has done so much for me? How can I live in the light of what He has done for me? I shouldn't be forgiven."

Think deeply about what Jesus has done for you. Ask yourself, what does that make me? What does that make Him to me? Now look at who lives inside you: the Holy Spirit. Grasping a true spiritual understanding of what He has done for you changes everything. You are walking around with the Holy Spirit inside you! How amazing is that!

Tell this story to yourself. Tell it to yourself again and again until it sinks into your understanding, until you grasp at a deep level what He has done and who He is in your life. "Therefore, if anyone is in Christ, he is a new creation. The old has passed away; behold, the new has come" (2 Cor. 5:17).

If Christ has set you free, you are free indeed. Nothing is more exciting, more freeing, more spectacular than knowing deep down to your toes that you are forgiven. Truly and utterly forgiven. And someone who knows they are forgiven walks and talks differently than someone who is still wondering if they are forgiven or not.

John Piper says this about how to live out the reality of being forgiven:

The best way to live out the reality of your forgiveness is to be stunned that you are a recipient of mercy—be reminded and stunned that you and I deserve nothing but wrath from God, and in Christ receive nothing but mercy from him. Be stunned. And then pray that God would bring this attitude into every moment of your every day.

Oh, how sweet marriages would be if we stopped thinking about what we deserve and thought more about how to show more mercy—how to do more undeserved good to each other. Oh, how sweet would be the fellowship of the church if we all really felt undeserving of any good and lavished with God's mercy. And, oh, how bright the gospel would shine if we touched the poor with Christ-exalting mercy. May God raise up many who will build, with joy, ministries of mercy to the city and the nations.[1]

1 John Piper. *"Are You Stunned That Your Sins Are Forgiven?"* DesiringGod.org. Desiring God Ministries. Web. 29 June 2016

I have to tell you about our Bible study last night. We were talking about grace and how it impacted us personally. You need to know that this is a group of missionaries sitting around, because you know, we missionaries have it all figured out.

It was truly a sacred moment as one friend shared about how she had struggled her whole life, thinking she was a Christian, but struggling alone, as she didn't understand that God's forgiveness was truly for her. She could grasp the idea of forgiveness but couldn't put it into her own life for herself. She described that this past year she had a breakthrough. She was so excited because she finally understood, for the first time, how simple it was. Simple. She had been trying to make it so difficult, so arduous, but the gospel, forgiveness, is so simple. She told us how now she just takes what God says at face value and chooses to believe it. That's all. And it has changed everything. When those feelings crop up of not feeling good enough, she just says, "Nope. I'm forgiven! That's enough. God forgave me and I'm His beloved child." And when she sins, she looks at that sin and says something like, "Oh, hang on, what's going on here. What am I feeling? Jealousy. I'm jealous of that person over there. I'm sorry, Lord. Thank You for forgiveness." And that's it! She is free to believe in her heart and her mind that she is truly forgiven!

A few other testimonies were given, all saying the same thing. How could so many of us have missed the simplicity of the beauty of forgiveness for this long?

As for myself, you will read more about my story in the next chapter, but we will start here. I am the firstborn daughter of a pastor of a large church. I have always had a deep love for God, for Christ, and a passion to serve Him. I prayed to ask the Lord to forgive me when I was eight. I walked forward at a camp to commit my life to being a missionary when I was twelve. I went on missions trips every summer, from junior high through high school, and then I went to college to study international missions. My goal was to end up single, living in a mud hut in Papua, New Guinea.

Obviously, God had other ideas, as I'm now married and the mother of six! But anyway, I have looked good. I have kept it together. I have made my parents proud. I have loved the Lord and told others about Him. But you know what was missing all those years? Freedom. Understanding grace. Understanding true forgiveness. It wasn't until the last five years of my life that I have begun to truly understand what forgiveness truly is and that I qualify for it. You see, I have always lived under this feeling of no matter how much I do, it's not enough. That I can do more. That I should do more. Comparing myself to others, maybe even to big-name speakers or missionaries, and think, I should be doing that. Or at least doing more. And whatever I've given up, or done, or sacrificed, it's never been enough, in my mind.

And then God gave me lupus. Lupus is the friend I never wanted and, frankly, hated with a passion. She was the one that held me back from going, going, going and doing, doing, doing. She's the one that still today says, "You will have a rest each and every day, and if you overdo it, you will be in bed for the next two days." And I've always looked at lupus as a curse, but God showed me it was a gift...and a gateway to understanding God's forgiveness.

For me, understanding forgiveness has been realizing I am so forgiven and so loved that it doesn't matter if I do absolutely nothing for God from now until the end of my time on earth; it doesn't change one, single thing. He doesn't care if I sit and stare at the wall, speak before thousands, or adopt twenty children. He loves me the same, and His forgiveness is the same in each case. I know this sounds simple, but to me it has been profound. To truly grasp at heart level that God's forgiveness is there no matter what, and nothing I do or don't do changes it, is true freedom.

How about you? Where are you in this journey? Are you struggling to grasp the truths of forgiveness? Are you longing to be free? Maybe you are like me or my friend who shared, you have known all about forgiveness for your whole life but haven't taken the step of just believing it? If that is you, I invite you to join me in tasting freedom.

Here is what I want you to do for me right now. Grab your Bible and your journal. Get a cup of something warm (or cold if you live in Africa like me!). Sit quietly for a few moments and ask God to show you through His Word, through the verses in this chapter and the chapters before what forgiveness really is and what it means in your life. If you are struggling to keep focused, try just thanking Him for what He's done: "Thank You, God; thank You, God." Ask Him for the faith and the belief to truly grasp at heart level the forgiveness that is yours. Stay there. Sit with Him. Make this a sacred moment of understanding between Him and you.

Now, take this into your every day. Like my friend, choose to believe it, and when those feelings come, when those thoughts come, speak truth over them. Declare that *you are forgiven*. Because you are. Declare that *you are loved*. Because you are.

When you sin, ask for His forgiveness, and then move on. Don't dwell on the past sins of today, last week, last month, or last year. Those are gone. They are covered, and you are forgiven. Walk in that today. And then tomorrow. And the day after that. It will be challenging at first, but like everything, with practice, as you do it again and again it will get easier until one day you will really and truly understand and believe that *you are forgiven*.

PRAYER

Heavenly Father, thank You for the many blessings that come as a result of our forgiveness in Jesus Christ. We are new creations; the old has passed away and the new has come. We praise You that our old self was crucified with Christ in order that our body of sin might be done away with. We are no longer slaves to sin but have been set free through Christ's finished work on the cross. In the name of our precious Lord and Savior, Jesus. Amen.

JOAN'S TESTIMONY

I spent most of my life wishing it could have been different. I'd been in the homes of many of my friends growing up, and I could see their families were nothing like mine. I'd often wished I had a different family and wondered why God put me where He did. Although I loved my family, I couldn't come to terms with my childhood, and when the physical abuse continued into my teen years, my feeling of injustice filled me with anger and bitterness.

I received the last beating at age thirteen. No laws mandated the reporting of child abuse. And many parents of that era shared the same views of corporal punishment.

Teachers turned a blind eye, and often extended family members were even unaware of what went on behind closed doors. We were weaned on secrecy and silence, so to tell anyone about the beatings would have been a betrayal that would not be tolerated.

I was taken to the doctor by my mother after a worse-than-normal beating. She was told if my father beat me like that again he might kill me. He explained both parents would be jailed, my father for perpetrating the abuse and she for allowing it to happen. That conversation became the catalyst for the divorce, which at that time was a scandal. We were shunned by the neighbors, and their children were prohibited from coming to our home. I had just become a teen, so losing my friends represented one more rejection I had to face in a trauma-filled life.

I spent the better part of my young adult life trying to fill my empty soul with people, places, and things. I left home when I was seventeen years old. I was fortunate to find a job that enabled me to support myself and began my quest for happiness. It's been said, sin takes you further than you want to go, keeps you longer than you want to stay, and costs you more than you want to pay. Sadly, I found this to be true.

I sought counsel from a religious leader and a mental health professional, hoping someone would help me come to terms with my childhood pain and my dysfunctional adult choices. In the end, all they could do was validate my feelings and stopped short of knowing how to help me resolve them. The root of bitterness grew unabated, and although I hated this attitude, my self-pity was my way of paying homage to my lost childhood.

I married my best friend of ten years. Yes, it does happen! We had two beautiful children, and I had hoped that fulfilling my dreams of having a wonderful husband and a family of my own would give me the peace that I'd been searching for. Unfortunately, I was still plagued with an overshadowing spirit of discontent that vexed me continually.

My life changed when a dear relative invited me to join her at church one Sunday morning. I heard God's plan of salvation, and I accepted Jesus Christ as my Savior. I was spiritually reborn on that day. My conversion was dramatic. As I began to read the Bible and learn of God's love for me, my heart began to soften. I began to forgive myself for the sin in my own life and saw the need to forgive others as well.

By now, my aging father was no longer able to care for himself and was living in a nursing home. I visited him often, and as I began to grow in my faith would share what God was doing in my life. He never said much; mostly he just listened.

One day our conversation turned serious, and I confessed the depth of bitterness and resentment I felt toward him because of my painful childhood. I explained that throughout the years I had shared with people the agony of those years, and as a result many were negatively influenced by my words. As a consequence, I didn't hold him in high regard. I asked him to forgive me, because I felt I had slandered his character and was wrong for doing so, despite the maltreatment I received by him.

I was not prepared for what was to come next. My intent had been to purge my conscience and walk in obedience to Jesus by asking for my father's forgiveness. But as soon as I made my confession, he said he forgave me and said he himself had suffered enormously throughout the years when he thought about the years of abuse. He said he had been plagued by nightmares and wished he could have been a different father. His countenance exposed the depth of his own torment, and my heart was broken. I verbally told him I forgave him and encouraged him to find the freedom for his tortured soul by asking Jesus to forgive him and cleanse him from his sin. With quivering lips and tear filled eyes, my father prayed. We held hands, cried together, and experienced a cleansing in our spirits and souls. Later, my husband explained the plan of salvation to my father, and Dad received Jesus as his personal Lord and Savior.

Old habits are often hard to break. At times after that beautiful encounter, I was tempted to be angry with my father for his past sin. I realized that anger and resentment were long-time residents in my life and were not easily uprooted. It was during those moments that the Holy Spirit reminded me my father had sincerely and humbly asked for my forgiveness, and I had verbally forgiven him. I resisted the temptation to allow my heart to return to a place of unforgiveness, and after consistently reminding myself that my father was forgiven by me and by God, the feeling of forgiveness slowly followed.

The Lord gave me and my dad a deep and tender love for one another. I couldn't have imagined that day would ever come, but God made it so. When I pondered our restored relationship, this scripture came to mind: "I will repay you for the years the locusts have eaten" (Joel 2:25 NIV).

Before my father died, I was allowed to see the depth to which God had apprehended his heart. Once I went to the nursing home and found Dad attending a midweek chapel service. Unaware of my presence, he sat in his wheelchair, tears on his face and singing the words to the song "Nothing but the Blood of Jesus." The memory is forever etched in my mind.

Who but God could have made that happen? My father was a new creation. The old had passed away; behold, he was made new in Christ!

I know many others love the Lord but have not experienced restoration or reconciliation with someone who may have hurt them in some way. I don't know why I was so blessed, and I certainly didn't do anything to deserve such a gift from God. But I continually praise Him for this treasure and cherish it in my heart always. I do know this: whether our offender asks for our forgiveness or not, we need to forgive out of an act of obedience to God. We must forgive as He forgave us. Forgiveness is not saying what happened to us was acceptable on any level. No, it is saying we are leaving the injustice with God, our Advocate.

If you forgive others their trespasses, your heavenly Father will also forgive you.

(Matt. 6:14)

Bearing with one another and, if one has a complaint against another, forgiving each other, as the Lord has forgiven you, so you also must forgive.

(Col. 3:13)

Monday

READ: 2 Corinthians 5

SOAP: 2 Corinthians 5:17

Scripture - Write out the **Scripture** passage for the day.

Observations - Write down 1 or 2 **observations** from the passage.

Monday

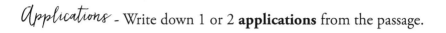

Applications - Write down 1 or 2 **applications** from the passage.

Pray - Write out a **prayer** over what you learned from today's passage.

-Visit our website today for the corresponding blog post!-

Tuesday

READ: Romans 12:1-2
SOAP: Romans 12:2

Scripture - Write out the **Scripture** passage for the day.

Observations - Write down 1 or 2 **observations** from the passage.

Tuesday

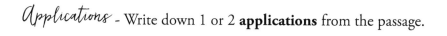

Applications - Write down 1 or 2 **applications** from the passage.

Pray - Write out a **prayer** over what you learned from today's passage.

Wednesday

READ: Romans 6:1-10
SOAP: Romans 6:6

Scripture - Write out the **Scripture** passage for the day.

Observations - Write down 1 or 2 **observations** from the passage.

Wednesday

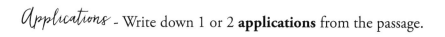

Applications - Write down 1 or 2 **applications** from the passage.

Pray - Write out a **prayer** over what you learned from today's passage.

-Visit our website today for the corresponding blog post!-

Thursday

READ: Colossians 3:1-17
SOAP: Colossians 3:1-3

Scripture - Write out the **Scripture** passage for the day.

Observations - Write down 1 or 2 **observations** from the passage.

Thursday

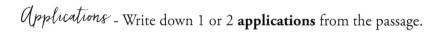

Applications - Write down 1 or 2 **applications** from the passage.

Pray - Write out a **prayer** over what you learned from today's passage.

Friday

READ: 1 John 5:1-4
SOAP: 1 John 5:4

Scripture - Write out the **Scripture** passage for the day.

Observations - Write down 1 or 2 **observations** from the passage.

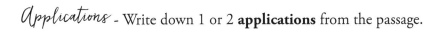
Applications - Write down 1 or 2 **applications** from the passage.

Pray - Write out a **prayer** over what you learned from today's passage.

-Visit our website today for the corresponding blog post!-

Reflection Questions

1. As a new creation in Christ, praise God for the many blessings that you now possess.

2. Think about Jesus' willingness to take the punishment for the sins you've committed. Tell Him how this makes you feel, giving Him the gratitude and praise He deserves.

3. Is there someone in your life whom you need to forgive? Pray to be obedient in this area.

4. Thank God for restoring a relationship with someone that you believed was beyond redemption.

5. Praise God for the gift of forgiveness, and pray to always keep "short accounts" with God, which is, confessing your sins quickly and receiving the forgiveness He graciously offers.

My Response

Week 5

Week 5 Challenge (Note: You can find this listed in our Monday blog post):

Prayer focus for this week: Spend time praying for missionaries.

	Praying	Praise
Monday		
Tuesday		
Wednesday		
Thursday		
Friday		

"Do not

be overcome by evil.

but overcome evil

with good".

ROMAS 12:21

Scripture for Week 5

MONDAY   *COLOSSIANS 3:12-14 (ESV)*

[12] Put on then, as God's chosen ones, holy and beloved, compassionate hearts, kindness, humility, meekness, and patience, [13] bearing with one another and, if one has a complaint against another, forgiving each other; as the Lord has forgiven you, so you also must forgive. [14] And above all these put on love, which binds everything together in perfect harmony.

TUESDAY   *MATTHEW 18:21-35 (ESV)*

[21] Then Peter came up and said to him, "Lord, how often will my brother sin against me, and I forgive him? As many as seven times?" [22] Jesus said to him, "I do not say to you seven times, but seventy-seven times.

[23] "Therefore the kingdom of heaven may be compared to a king who wished to settle accounts with his servants. [24] When he began to settle, one was brought to him who owed him ten thousand talents. [25] And since he could not pay, his master ordered him to be sold, with his wife and children and all that he had, and payment to be made. [26] So the servant fell on his knees, imploring him, 'Have patience with me, and I will pay you everything.' [27] And out of pity for him, the master of that servant released him and forgave him the debt. [28] But when that same servant went out, he found one of his fellow servants who owed him a hundred denarii, and seizing him, he began to choke him, saying, 'Pay what you owe.' [29] So his fellow servant fell down and pleaded with him, 'Have patience with me, and I will pay you.' [30] He refused and went and put him in prison until he should pay the debt. [31] When his fellow servants saw what had taken place, they were greatly distressed, and they went and reported to their master all that had taken place. [32] Then his master summoned him and said to him, 'You wicked servant! I forgave you all that debt because you pleaded with me. [33] And should not you have had mercy on your

fellow servant, as I had mercy on you?' [34] And in anger his master delivered him to the jailers, until he should pay all his debt. [35] So also my heavenly Father will do to every one of you, if you do not forgive your brother from your heart."

WEDNESDAY   *ROMANS 12:17-21 (ESV)*

[17] Repay no one evil for evil, but give thought to do what is honorable in the sight of all. [18] If possible, so far as it depends on you, live peaceably with all. [19] Beloved, never avenge yourselves, but leave it to the wrath of God, for it is written, "Vengeance is mine, I will repay, says the Lord." [20] To the contrary, "if your enemy is hungry, feed him; if he is thirsty, give him something to drink; for by so doing you will heap burning coals on his head." [21] Do not be overcome by evil, but overcome evil with good.

THURSDAY   *MARK 11:20-25 (ESV)*

[20] As they passed by in the morning, they saw the fig tree withered away to its roots. [21] And Peter remembered and said to him, "Rabbi, look! The fig tree that you cursed has withered."[22] And Jesus answered them, "Have faith in God. [23] Truly, I say to you, whoever says to this mountain, 'Be taken up and thrown into the sea,' and does not doubt in his heart, but believes that what he says will come to pass, it will be done for him. [24] Therefore I tell you, whatever you ask in prayer, believe that you have received it, and it will be yours. [25] And whenever you stand praying, forgive, if you have anything against anyone, so that your Father also who is in heaven may forgive you your trespasses."

FRIDAY

[9] Pray then like this:

"Our Father in heaven,

hallowed be your name.

[10] Your kingdom come,

your will be done,

on earth as it is in heaven.

[11] Give us this day our daily bread,

[12] and forgive us our debts,

as we also have forgiven our debtors.

[13] And lead us not into temptation,

but deliver us from evil.

5

THE CALL OF FORGIVENESS

BY JOY FORNEY

SHE WALKED IN with her shoulders slumped and her head hung low, and I was livid. My sister had run off the week I was leaving with my family of five for Indonesia, and then the day of our departure she sauntered back in. As I told you in my previous chapter, I am the oldest daughter of a pastor of a large church. I'm the smiley, perfect one who keeps it all together and makes everyone look good. I was leaving to become a missionary—pretty much the highest accolades you are allowed to get in the Christian world. I was the superstar, the one who always made us look good. And she wasn't. And she was stealing my show. And I was mad.

My sister, four years younger than I am, had always been a free spirit. She was the one who really didn't care what others thought, and I wanted her to care...and I tried to make her care. And through a culmination of events and stresses, she ran off to a bit of a wild life during the week that was supposed to be all about me. *Ahem*. I mean, all about God, of course.

My little family, my handsome pilot hubby, our three young children, and I were about to embark on a new adventure of becoming missionaries with Mission Aviation Fellowship in Indonesia. That week before we left was about packing and stocking up on things like chocolate chips, vanilla, and clothing for the next three and a half years. It was about us being prayed over in front of the large church, smiling out at the masses who would be praying for us. It was supposed to be a time of lasts. The last Taco Bell burrito, last drive through the beautiful Columbia Gorge, last goodbyes. Instead, it was filled with worry over where my sister was, where she had gone, and whom she was with. It was spent combing through her e-mails and phone records trying to locate where she had gone. And then suddenly, the day we were leaving, she showed up. And in that moment, I wanted my dad to lay into her. I wanted him to let her know, loud and clear, what she had done to us, how we had worried, how she had wrecked our perfect family image, rained on my parade, and essentially royally messed up. And you know what he did instead? He sat down on the stoop beside the front door and put his arm around her shoulder and told her he was so glad she had come back. In her mess, her disaster of the week prior, he sat down and offered grace and forgiveness. And it is a picture I will never forget. However, although I wish I could say that I sat down on the other side of her, put my arm around her, and did the same, I did not. I eked out a tight-lipped good-bye and stewed and steamed all the way to Indonesia. I was not forgiving. I was not gracious. I told my story to those who would listen with pleas for sympathy on my behalf. I wanted people to understand how hard that was for me.

I was the "older brother" in the story of the prodigal son. For years, I have looked at that story as an amazing story of redemption and love between the younger son and the father. And it is. It is a beautiful picture of the wayward son returning and the father's extravagant forgiveness, a beautiful picture of what I witnessed that day on the stoop at my house.

More than that, it's the story of me, the older brother. The self-righteous Pharisee that thinks he is doing everything right, and when grace and forgiveness are offered he turns away in disgust. That's me. In the moment of redemption, of reconciliation, I had the opportunity to join the feast, to join the party and make merry. Instead, I turned away and rested in my goodness, my rightness, which sounded good at the time, but now looking back, all I can see are clanging cymbals and noisy gongs. Filthy rags. All of my efforts were like filthy rags (Isa.64:6).

I had been resting on my goodness, my appearance of having it all together, my self-righteousness, instead of the cross. I was a Pharisee. And this story of forgiveness isn't about me forgiving my sister for ruining my big show and stealing my spotlight; it is about the forgiveness that I needed to accept from Him.

Only when we realize and accept the radical forgiveness we are offered can we forgive ourselves and then extend that to others in our lives and live in the freedom of truly being forgiven. Freely, freely, you have received. Freely, freely give. And you would think that having been a Christian who prayed to ask Jesus into my heart way back when I was eight, I would have already figured this out. But the truth of this story is, while I did ask Jesus to forgive my sins and be my Lord and Savior, I didn't truly think I was all that bad. Possibly in my mind I was thinking I was sort of an asset to the team. That God somehow was kind of lucky to have me on His side. Yikes. Even writing those statements make me cringe. But God knew, and He was there waiting for me to realize just how far and deep and wide my sin truly went.

And looking at the picture that my dad showed in sitting down and putting his arm around my sister in the midst of her sin, that's the story I wanted with God. I wanted to confess my sin in its entirety, not covering up a thing, and have Him sit down in my mess and forgive me. "Therefore if anyone is in Christ, he is a new creation. The old has passed away; behold, the new has come" (2 Cor. 5:17).

The beauty of forgiveness from God is that no matter where you are in life, it is for you. It doesn't matter if you are my sister in the story, messing up in big and public ways. And it equally doesn't matter if you are me, the one who tried to keep it all together, looking good on the outside but on the inside full of sinful pride and selfishness. The act was the same and the result is the same. Christ died for all sinners, public and private, the ones who thought they needed him and the ones who thought they were doing pretty well on their own.

Once I truly grasped the idea that I was the sinner, with nothing good in and of myself, was I able to truly embrace the forgiveness given to me. And then extend that to those around me, including my little sister.

The apostle Peter asked Jesus how many times we allow others to sin against us and still choose to forgive. Peter asked him, "'Lord, how often will my brother sin against me, and I forgive him? As many as seven times?' Jesus said to him, 'I do not say to you seven times, but seventy-seven times'" (Matt. 18:21–22).

So let's walk through this story and understand how we not only can accept forgiveness but also extend it to others. The first step in truly understanding forgiveness is to know the absolute, unshakeable reality of God's love.

To really understand this kind of love, you have to move your thinking from a "God loves the whole world and me in it" view, seeing just the things He does to care for you and your family, to a new view. Those things like food and clothing are good, but that understanding stops short. I believe that is where I was stuck for most of my life, understanding that God loved me in a big, sweeping way. But that understanding limits not only God but our view of forgiveness.

No, the love that God has for us is the love a Father has for a child, a love that has Christ taking our place on the cross in death. It is the picture of my dad sitting down on the stoop with my sister. It's not a far-off love; it's a close, intimate, endearing, specific love.

If you doubt this truth or your place in it, look no further than the apostle Paul's letter where tells us that the love of God chose us for adoption as children of God. He chose us in Christ before the foundation of the world so we would be holy and blameless before Him. In love He adopted us as sons so we can call him Abba, Father" (Eph. 1:4–5). It is a love that is for you personally. God's love chose you and pursued you so deeply that you can't escape.

Take a moment and sit with the fact that God pursued you. You. He loved you so much that He took it upon Himself to make sure He had you together with Him. He stooped down and put that arm around you in the moment of your greatest shame. What is that moment? Go there for a minute. Yes, it is painful and uncomfortable. Think about your moment of greatest shame. And now picture God in His majesty, sitting down beside you and wrapping His arms around you…in that moment. Just stay there. Thank God for this. For loving you in the mess. For loving you when you didn't deserve it. For loving you when you thought you did deserve it, like I did. For loving you enough not to give up, even when you were pushing Him away. Feel the forgiveness. Accept the forgiveness. Relish and revel in the forgiveness.

Maybe take a moment to journal your thoughts to the Lord about what being forgiven does to your soul. How it makes you sing and how it helps you move from knowing you are forgiven to believing you are forgiven. This moment will shape the later moments. This moment takes the future of your understanding and acting out of forgiveness. This is the moment that changes all the moments to come. Without the depth of understanding of how truly, completely, utterly loved and forgiven you are, you can't truly understand how to offer that in your life and in the lives of others. So don't rush over these tender moments with God. Thank Him for His grace, for His mercy, for His love poured out on you, the vilest of sinners. "Jesus paid it all, All to Him I owe; Sin had left a crimson stain, He washed it white as snow." [Song is in public domain.]

Sometimes it's easy to picture God cheering for us, smiling at us in our big, spectacular happy success moments. The bright-lights stage moments when everything is going our way and we are feeling good about ourselves and our accomplishments. But God loved us in our worst moments too. In our icky, down and dirty, shameful moments. Whether you are my troubled sister or whether you are me, the moments are equally icky and disgusting.

Once you realize the breadth and depth and heights of what God did and what it cost Him, you will begin to see forgiving others in your life in a different way. Easy? Nope. But as we look at how loved and how forgiven we truly are, we can then look and see the ability and the need to forgive others in our life.

Is there someone in your life who needs your forgiveness? Is there someone in your life you've been holding a grudge against because it hurts too much to let it go? Is there someone in your life who has wronged you deeply, and the thought of letting it go feels too much like letting them off the hook?

Even though in my story my sister's sin against me was minimal, it did take time for me to forgive the hurt and the pain and the ugly words that were exchanged. I carried that wound like a badge. I was in the right and I had been wronged, so I was going to let everyone know that she was wrong. And that was wrong.

Paul let us know that we are to "be kind to one another, tenderhearted, forgiving one another, as God in Christ forgave you" (Eph. 4:32). Because Christ forgave us, it gives us the unnatural ability to do the same. This isn't a shaming thing, like, Christ did it, now you must… No. This is a deep understanding, feeling, and knowing deep in your soul that you are forgiven, and it breaks so many things loose in your heart and mind. It is a realization deep down to your toes that you have been forgiven much so, therefore, you can forgive much. It's a gift. Not to the other person but to yourself. It is an invitation to walk in love, just as Christ loved you. It is a beautiful picture of grace and love poured out on the person who has done you wrong.

We hear many stories of people who have been wronged horribly, and yet by God's grace and mercy they are able to forgive. Corrie ten Boom is one of them. Corrie and her sister Betsie were arrested and imprisoned for hiding Jews in their home when the Nazis occupied the Netherlands. Many years later while speaking on forgiveness, Corrie saw one of the guards from the time of her imprisonment. It's a lot to take in. Her sister had died in prison and she herself had suffered cruelly at the hands of the Nazis.

This is her story:

> That's when I saw him, working his way forward against the others. One moment I saw the overcoat and the brown hat; the next, a blue uniform and a visored cap with its skull and crossbones.
>
> It came back with a rush: the huge room with its harsh overhead lights, the pathetic pile of dresses and shoes in the center of the floor, the shame of walking naked past this man. I could see my sister's frail form ahead of me, ribs sharp beneath the parchment skin.
>
> This man had been a guard at Ravensbrück concentration camp where we were sent. Now he was in front of me, hand thrust out: "A fine message, *fräulein*! How good it is to know that, as you say, all our sins are at the bottom of the sea!"
>
> And I, who had spoken so glibly of forgiveness, fumbled in my pocketbook rather than take that hand. He would not remember me, of course—how could he remember one prisoner among those thousands of women? But I remembered him and the leather crop swinging from his belt. It was the first time since my release that I had been face to face with one of my captors and my blood seemed to freeze.
>
> "You mentioned Ravensbrück in your talk," he was saying. "I was

a guard in there." No, he did not remember me.

"But since that time," he went on, "I have become a Christian. I know that God has forgiven me for the cruel things I did there, but I would like to hear it from your lips as well. *Fräulein*"—again the hand came out—"will you forgive me?"

And I stood there—I whose sins had every day to be forgiven—and could not. Betsie had died in that place- could he erase her slow terrible death simply for the asking?

It could not have been many seconds that he stood there, hand held out, but to me it seemed hours as I wrestled with the most difficult thing I had ever had to do. For I had to do it—I knew that. The message that God forgives has a prior condition: that we forgive those who have injured us. "If you do not forgive men their trespasses," Jesus says, "neither will your Father in heaven forgive your trespasses." I knew it not only as a commandment of God, but as a daily experience.

Since the end of the war I had had a home in Holland for victims of Nazi brutality. Those who were able to forgive their former enemies were able also to return to the outside world and rebuild their lives, no matter what the physical scars. Those who nursed their bitterness remained invalids. It was as simple and as horrible as that.

And still I stood there with the coldness clutching my heart. But forgiveness is not an emotion—I knew that too. Forgiveness is an act of the will, and the will can function regardless of the temperature of the heart. "Jesus, help me!" I prayed silently. "I can lift my hand. I can do that much. You supply the feeling."

And so woodenly, mechanically, I thrust my hand into the one stretched out to me. And as I did, an incredible thing took place. The current started in my shoulder, raced down my arm, sprang into our joined hands. And then this healing warmth seemed to flood my whole being, bringing tears to my eyes. "I forgive you, brother!" I cried. "With all my heart!"[1]

Jesus came to save us so we can be truly free. And as He has forgiven us of so much, it frees us when we are able to then turn around and forgive those in our lives. It is not a simple thing. But as in Corrie's story, sometimes we just need to show up and do the right thing and let Him do the rest. To be available to hear and see the sin, the way out, and the way we should go. And let Him do the rest.

PRAYER

Heavenly Father, thank You for forgiving my many sins. Thank You for teaching me that as You have forgiven me, so must I forgive others. Thank You, Holy Spirit, for convicting my heart when self-righteousness and pride reign supreme in my life and allowing me to see my need for a Savior. In Jesus' name. Amen.

ANGI'S TESTIMONY

I held his hand, touched his hair and felt his beard. It was the first time I got to see and touch my dad. He was in a coma and didn't know I was there. He didn't get to tell me he was sorry or that he loved me. He would lie in the intensive care unit in critical condition for one week before my mom and siblings would give permission to take him off life support. It was a lot for my eleven-year-old brain to take in.

It seems my entire spiritual journey has been about forgiveness... forgiving myself and forgiving others. As a child I have no memories of seeing my dad. My parents divorced before I was three, and a restraining order forbade my dad from being near any of us. I was always told Dad couldn't come near us because he was sick with mental illness and alcoholism.

---

1   https://www.guideposts.org/inspiration/stories-of-hope/guideposts-classics-corrie-ten-boom-on-forgiveness?nopaging=1

Occasionally we would have a dad sighting. I have one vague memory of seeing him at a gas station, and when I asked my older siblings to let me go to him they said, "No," because he was sick and we just couldn't help him.

I was thirteen years old and in the seventh grade when I was introduced to marijuana. I began drinking heavily then got into cocaine as a junior in high school. I could have ended up in a different school system, but as I was in a special education class they worked with me continuously to succeed in school. I made an effort at sobriety during my senior year and left home one month after graduation. After working briefly at a gas station, I started working at a home- based daycare center and was living in subsidized housing.

After a friend died, I began the downward spiral once again. I really wanted to turn my life around but was still struggling when I conceived a child in October. I'd lost my housing and was living in a homeless shelter. My family encouraged me to birth my child and give her up through open adoption. I didn't want to do it. I cleaned up my act after the second month of pregnancy and carried my daughter to term. The moment I held her, I felt this was why I was born; I was meant to be a mother. My whole life changed. I promised to give her the life she deserved and not repeat the sins of my father. There and then began my journey to healing.

I moved in with my mom when my daughter was two months old. Through the pregnancy I got involved with a Youth for Christ teen pregnancy group. I hadn't accepted Jesus Christ as my Savior yet, but they were helping me along. They didn't force religion on me but talked about God's love while guiding me down the path toward Him. It was about two years later when I surrendered my life to Jesus, and everything turned around.

I asked God to forgive me for my bad choices and I began the process of forgiving myself and others. Three years ago I began a Bible study, started to learn more about the Bible, grew stronger in my knowledge of God, and joined a church.

My damaged emotions began to heal, and I knew I needed to forgive my father. His urn of ashes was in our home, and a few of his personal possessions were given to us by the homeless shelter he'd been living in prior to his death. Now years after his passing, I clutched the urn and some of his belongings in my arms, and I began to cry. I prayed a prayer of forgiveness, telling my father I forgave him for not being a part of my life. I forgave him for his addiction, and I was able to release the anger, bitterness, and resentment that I'd carried for so long. I believe my father wouldn't want me to hold onto those emotions, and I feel he'd be proud that I was able to move on and grow from my past.

One of the biggest things I take away from my experience is not to judge others. People have judged me my entire life, and it has broken me to pieces. I can always find sympathy for someone because I don't know what they've walked, where they have been, what they have suffered.

I've wanted to share how I got to Jesus through my life story. I hope to encourage others to allow Jesus to bring them to a place of forgiveness as well. People see me as strong, but my strength comes from being forgiven, forgiving myself, and forgiving others.

- - - - - - -

He has delivered us from the domain of darkness and transferred us to the kingdom of his beloved Son, in whom we have redemption, the forgiveness of sins.

(Col. 1:13–14)

Monday

READ: Colossians 3:12-14

SOAP: Colossians 3:13

Scripture - Write out the **Scripture** passage for the day.

Observations - Write down 1 or 2 **observations** from the passage.

YOU ARE FORGIVEN

Monday

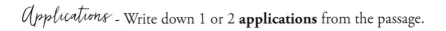

Applications - Write down 1 or 2 **applications** from the passage.

Pray - Write out a **prayer** over what you learned from today's passage.

-Visit our website today for the corresponding blog post!-

Tuesday

READ: Matthew 18:21-35

SOAP: Matthew 18:21-22

Scripture - Write out the **Scripture** passage for the day.

Observations - Write down 1 or 2 **observations** from the passage.

Tuesday

Applications - Write down 1 or 2 **applications** from the passage.

Pray - Write out a **prayer** over what you learned from today's passage.

Wednesday

READ: Romans 12:17-21
SOAP: Romans 12:21

Scripture - Write out the **Scripture** passage for the day.

Observations - Write down 1 or 2 **observations** from the passage.

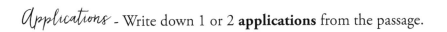

Applications - Write down 1 or 2 **applications** from the passage.

Pray - Write out a **prayer** over what you learned from today's passage.

-Visit our website today for the corresponding blog post!-

READ: Mark 11:20-25
SOAP: Mark 11:25

Scripture - Write out the **Scripture** passage for the day.

Observations - Write down 1 or 2 **observations** from the passage.

Thursday

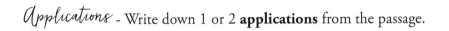

Applications - Write down 1 or 2 **applications** from the passage.

Pray - Write out a **prayer** over what you learned from today's passage.

Friday

READ: Matthew 6:9-13
SOAP: Matthew 6:12-13

Scripture - Write out the **Scripture** passage for the day.

Observations - Write down 1 or 2 **observations** from the passage.

YOU ARE FORGIVEN

Friday

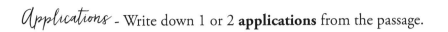

Applications - Write down 1 or 2 **applications** from the passage.

Pray - Write out a **prayer** over what you learned from today's passage.

-Visit our website today for the corresponding blog post!-

Reflection Questions

1. Has someone you know asked and received God's forgiveness that you didn't feel deserved to be forgiven?

2. Think of a time when a self-righteous attitude made you think you were more virtuous than someone else. What did God do to show you your own sinful attitude?

3. Have you witnessed someone forgive another to the degree that it humbled and broke you, showing you your own self-centeredness and pride?

4. Do you struggle accepting the absolute, unshakable reality of the depth of God's love for you? If so, pray that God would allow you to receive His love with joy.

5. Have you ever had a Corrie ten Boom experience, whereby you hesitated to extend forgiveness to someone, but once you stepped out in obedience God met you there and gave you the ability to truly forgive?

My Response

Week 6

Week 6 Challenge (Note: You can find this listed in our Monday blog post):

Prayer focus for this week: Spend time praying for you.

	Praying	Praise
Monday		
Tuesday		
Wednesday		
Thursday		
Friday		

YOU ARE FORGIVEN

But thanks be to God!
He gives us the victory through
our Lord Jesus Christ.

1 CORINTHIANS 15:57

Scripture for Week 6

MONDAY

Of David.

¹⁰³ Bless the Lord, O my soul,
  and all that is within me,
  bless his holy name!
² Bless the Lord, O my soul,
  and forget not all his benefits,
³ who forgives all your iniquity,
  who heals all your diseases,
⁴ who redeems your life from the pit,
  who crowns you with steadfast love and mercy,
⁵ who satisfies you with good
  so that your youth is renewed like the eagle's.
⁶ The Lord works righteousness
  and justice for all who are oppressed.
⁷ He made known his ways to Moses,
  his acts to the people of Israel.
⁸ The Lord is merciful and gracious,
  slow to anger and abounding in steadfast love.
⁹ He will not always chide,
  nor will he keep his anger forever.
¹⁰ He does not deal with us according to our sins,
  nor repay us according to our iniquities.
¹¹ For as high as the heavens are above the earth,
  so great is his steadfast love toward those who fear him;
¹² as far as the east is from the west,

so far does he remove our transgressions from us.

¹³ As a father shows compassion to his children,

so the Lord shows compassion to those who fear him.

¹⁴ For he knows our frame;

he remembers that we are dust.

¹⁵ As for man, his days are like grass;

he flourishes like a flower of the field;

¹⁶ for the wind passes over it, and it is gone,

and its place knows it no more.

¹⁷ But the steadfast love of the Lord is from everlasting to everlasting on those who fear him,

and his righteousness to children's children,

¹⁸ to those who keep his covenant

and remember to do his commandments.

¹⁹ The Lord has established his throne in the heavens,

and his kingdom rules over all.

²⁰ Bless the Lord, O you his angels,

you mighty ones who do his word,

obeying the voice of his word!

²¹ Bless the Lord, all his hosts,

his ministers, who do his will!

²² Bless the Lord, all his works,

in all places of his dominion.

Bless the Lord, O my soul!

TUESDAY   *1 CORINTHIANS 15:50-57 (ESV)*

⁵⁰ I tell you this, brothers: flesh and blood cannot inherit the kingdom of God, nor does the perishable inherit the imperishable. ⁵¹ Behold! I tell you a mystery. We shall not all sleep, but we shall all be changed, ⁵² in a moment, in the twinkling of an eye, at the last trumpet. For the trumpet will sound, and the dead will be raised imperishable, and we shall be changed. ⁵³ For this perishable body must put on the imperishable, and this mortal body must put on immortality. ⁵⁴ When the perishable puts on the imperishable, and the mortal puts on immortality, then shall come to pass the saying that is written:

"Death is swallowed up in victory."

⁵⁵ "O death, where is your victory?

O death, where is your sting?"

⁵⁶ The sting of death is sin, and the power of sin is the law. ⁵⁷ But thanks be to God, who gives us the victory through our Lord Jesus Christ.

WEDNESDAY   *LUKE 17:11-19 (ESV)*

¹¹ On the way to Jerusalem he was passing along between Samaria and Galilee. ¹² And as he entered a village, he was met by ten lepers, who stood at a distance ¹³ and lifted up their voices, saying, "Jesus, Master, have mercy on us." ¹⁴ When he saw them he said to them, "Go and show yourselves to the priests." And as they went they were cleansed. ¹⁵ Then one of them, when he saw that he was healed, turned back, praising God with a loud voice; ¹⁶ and he fell on his face at Jesus' feet, giving him thanks. Now he was a Samaritan. ¹⁷ Then Jesus answered, "Were not ten cleansed? Where are the nine? ¹⁸ Was no one found to return and give praise to God except this foreigner?" ¹⁹ And he said to him, "Rise and go your way; your faith has made you well."

THURSDAY

[20] This is the gate of the Lord;

the righteous shall enter through it.

[21] I thank you that you have answered me

and have become my salvation.

[22] The stone that the builders rejected

has become the cornerstone.

[23] This is the Lord's doing;

it is marvelous in our eyes.

[24] This is the day that the Lord has made;

let us rejoice and be glad in it.

FRIDAY

[20] giving thanks always and for everything to God the Father in the name of our Lord Jesus Christ,

6

THE FRUIT OF OUR FORGIVENESS
PART 1: GRATITUDE

BY ANGELA PERRITT

Grace for Super Mom

I HAD ALLOWED my life to become a little too busy. It was Christmastime and two of my three daughters were each involved in separate Christmas pageants across town. In my best "I Can Do It, I'm Super Mom" attitude, I strategically came up with the best plan to attend each daughter's Christmas program and felt pretty proud of myself, I must say.

The night started off without a hitch. I got Addie to the church in time for her run-through and then drove to the middle school to drop off my preschooler for her first-ever Christmas pageant. She was super excited and so was I.

Arriving early, I was able to grab the best seats in the house, right in the center, perfect view of the whole stage. It didn't matter where Brinnley would be standing; with my video camera and stills, I'd be able to videotape the whole thing!

I was so proud of my super-mom skills, up until the time the preschool slideshow began. As picture after picture flashed across the screen, I realized that, unlike with my older two daughters, I had missed out on some class parties and activities this past year with my youngest. My heart began to sink as picture after picture showed mothers and daughters icing cookies together, playing games, and posing for pictures. As I watched, my heart began to break with each click of the next slide. By the time the slide show was over, I was holding back the tears…and seriously rethinking the strategy between making it to both performances.

Looking at the program, Brin's class was scheduled right in the middle of the performance. No problem, I thought. Instead of making just one of her songs, I think I can stay a little longer and watch both her class's song and dances. I mean, seriously, how could I not? The guilt I was experiencing with already missing out had me almost in tears. No way could I leave early now!

And honestly, my clever little plan would have worked…if the school hadn't scheduled parent testimonies right before my daughter's class! What should have been maybe five or ten minutes, ended up being three families, each sharing how wonderful the school was for their children, how prepared their children were for kindergarten…on and on and on for about thirty minutes.

I was dying in my seat! I already knew the time between both performances was close, but this was just painful! How could I leave one daughter without seeing any of her Christmas pageant, and yet how could I not be there for another?

Looking at my watch, I estimated that I had just enough time to watch Brin's class, grab her from her teachers as soon as her tiny feet left the stage to haul out and race to the church just in time for Addie's song. Surely I'd have a good twenty to twenty-five minutes before Addie's turn.

After grabbing Brinnley from her teachers, I "put the pedal to the metal" in my car and literally ran into the church. As I flung open the doors and raced to the seats with Brin on my hip, because I wasn't waiting around for her little legs to catch up with mine, I realized to my horror that I had miscalculated, and the kids were singing the last song of their Christmas pageant!

I had missed Addie's whole performance! I missed her parts that we had rehearsed together, her duet and her dancing. I had missed it all.

And she knew it.

She saw me run into the room from where she stood on stage.

My "Super Mom" banner fell lifelessly to the floor.

I had failed.

Oh how my heart hurt as I realized I had missed it all! The thought of Addie being on stage and my not being in the audience was too much to handle, and tears began streaming down my face. I honestly tried to hold myself together as I embraced her when the program was over and the cast had finished taking their pictures. But I just couldn't. I had to excuse myself and go into the women's bathroom to cry it out for a few minutes. The shame, regret; it was just too much to hold in.

That night I kneeled next to Addie's bed, and with tears filling up my eyes again, I asked her to forgive me for missing her play. I really messed up. I tried to be more than I was. I'm not super mom after all.

Addie sat up in her bed, draped her arms around my neck and whispered, "It's okay Mommy. I know you tried your best. I saw you running into the room. You tried your hardest. I forgive you, just like you forgive me when I mess up. We forgive each other."

And just like that, she gave me a kiss on the cheek, lay back in bed, and rolled over to go to sleep.

I learned a priceless lesson on forgiveness that night from my sweet Addie. It feels good to be forgiven. No matter how hard we try, no matter how super we think we can be, we all miss the mark from time to time. Life is messy and disappointing, and at times we hurt those we never intend to. And that's where grace and forgiveness come into play.

Addie could have told me how disappointed she was in me. She could have told me how unfair it was that all the other kids had their moms there and she didn't. She could have tried to hurt me back. But she didn't. She chose to forgive and extend compassion instead.

God does the same.

"He does not deal with us according to our sins, nor repay us according to our iniquities. For as high as the heavens are above the earth, so great is his steadfast love toward those who fear him" (Ps. 103:10–11).

His loving-kindness toward us is immeasurable, for how can one measure where heaven begins?

Because of our sins we deserve death, we deserve wrath, but instead God gives us Jesus. And through Jesus, we have forgiveness of sin and eternal life.

We deserve hell, and God gives us heaven in its place. God sees all we do. He sees us mess up and miss Christmas pageants, games, and birthdays. He sees us come short, run late into school programs, and miss important meetings. And yet He chooses to extend loving-kindness and forgiveness instead of judgment and wrath.

In Psalm 103 we get an amazing glimpse into the heart of our loving, forgiving Father. We read that He forgives all our sins, heals our diseases, redeems our lives from the pit, crowns us with love and compassion, and satisfies our desires with good things (Ps. 103:3–5). We learn that God is compassionate and gracious, slow to anger and abounding in love (v. 8). That He has removed our sins as far as east is from west. In other words, He has removed them from us forever, because east and west never meet. When God says he forgives us our sins, He means it (v. 12).

We're totally, completely forgiven. "As a father has compassion on his children, so the LORD has compassion on those who fear him; for he knows how we are formed, he remembers that we are dust" (Ps. 103:13–14 NIV).

My three girls are blessed with an amazing dad. I knew my husband, Dirk, was going to be a great dad when I married him, but he has surpassed even my extremely high expectations. My husband adores our girls, and it shows in how he loves them. Dirk delights in spending time with them. Just running out on a Saturday morning to do some last-minute errands with one of our girls brings him so much joy. I can't tell you how many times he will come back with one of them or all three of them to tell me how proud he is of our girls, how much he loves them, and then proceeds to fill me in on the funny things they talked about as they went around town going to the hardware store, the local garden center, or grocery store. What they are doing or where they are going doesn't matter to him; what he loves is just the time he gets to spend with them.

I share all this because when I read verses like Psalm 103:13–14, I see a picture of my husband and our girls. I know my husband dearly loves our girls; he would lay his life down for them in a heartbeat. And yet Dirk is human. And though I think he is the best dad ever, he, too, just like the rest of us, has flaws, has made mistakes, and needs forgiveness. Yet no matter how much my husband loves our girls, it can never even come close to how much God loves each and every one of us. So though we may not all have been blessed with a loving and supportive earthly father like my girls have, we all share the same amazing heavenly Father who loves us and takes into account our weaknesses!

A few months ago, I read a story by Max Lucado, one of my favorite authors, about a person who brought Max and his wife, Denalyn, a lot of stress. This individual was, at times, demanding and quite rude. Without reason she would scream at them in public and harass them in the middle of the night, causing Max and his wife to get little sleep for months. But despite the mistreatment, they chose to love her instead, to comfort her as best they could, and tend to the needs they knew about. They never told her to leave them alone or to go find someone else to bother. After all, she was their daughter, and she was only a few months old.

Like God, Max and his wife had compassion on their infant daughter and took into account their daughter's limitations. God does the same for us. He knows our backgrounds; he knows our limitations. After all, He made us. He knows our fragility. After all, we are but dust (Ps. 103:14).

Let's embrace the fact that our God loves us like a compassionate father, knows our sins, and yet chooses to forgive us of our sins. He not only forgives us, but removes our sins from us as far as east is from west. Our Father understands we are but dust and knows our limitations. How should we respond to such extravagant love?

With gratitude.

God's choice to forgive and extend love to us should result in our choosing to accept His forgiveness and live lives characterized by gratitude! Though we are weak and made of dust, we are strong because of Him. Remember that "he who is in you is greater than he who is in the world" (1 John 4:4).

Accept the forgiveness that God so lovingly extends. No longer can Satan accuse you of your past sins. If you have accepted Jesus Christ as your Lord and Savior, Satan has no power over you and your life (John 8:36). Because of Jesus and the saving work He did on the cross, we now have victory over our sins, over our failures, over our past. Cling to that truth, and the next time Satan reminds you of your past, you remind him of his future!

In Luke 17 Jesus told the story of ten men, dirty and skinny from lack of food, and sick, very sick with leprosy. These men were outcasts. Not allowed in with the others, they were labeled "unclean," sick, and posed a serious threat to the rest of the community if they were to be included with those who were considered "clean." Their disease could contaminate others, and so they must be removed.

How long these men were outcasts we do not know. What they left behind—jobs, houses, friends, and family—we are not told. What we do know is they were desperate to get back to their lives and what was lost due to that horrible disease. And so they took a gamble; what did they have to lose? They had heard about this Jesus and how He was healing those like them, making the blind see and the crippled walk. Maybe, just maybe this Jesus could help them too. And so with nothing to lose, they stood at a distance and shouted with all their might, "Jesus, Master, have mercy on us!" (v. 13)

And Jesus turned and looked at them. The God of heaven who came down and walked in human form, looked at them.

He saw them (v. 14).

He saw them in their diseased state. He saw their helplessness, their appearance, and their longing to once again be healthy and whole, to once again be "clean." And so He responded to their plea, saying, "Go, show yourselves to the priests" (v. 14).

What I absolutely love about this story is how God healed them "as they went" (v. 14). As they literally walked their faith out in obedience, step by step, they were cleansed.

Can you even imagine? At first they might have thought Jesus was blowing them off. "What do you mean show ourselves to the priests? In this state? You've got to be kidding!" But what did they have to lose? Maybe this was a minor detail that whoever had told them about Jesus forgot to share. So all ten of them moved forward, step by step, one foot after another, walking forward in obedience, hoping for the best but not sure of it just yet.

And then with each step, their strength began to come back, and with that their desire to take one more step forward. Soon the healing that was taking place internally began to appear outwardly as well. With each step forward the disease took one step back, until all ten were finally healed. Ten men who had lost everything were given a second chance at life, thanks to Jesus!

Yet the surprising twist to this story is not that Jesus healed them with each step of their journey back home, but that only one of the ten came back to thank the One who provided the healing.

Only one.

Nine of the ten took the healing for granted. Nine of the ten allowed Jesus to heal them physically but not spiritually, for only one learned the source of his healing: his faith.

So what about you, sweet friend? Have you accepted God's forgiveness in your life? If so, don't be one of the nine who goes on with life forgiven but without gratitude. God has done an amazing work in all of our lives, and we should live lives characterized by gratitude because of the forgiveness Jesus has bestowed upon us!

So what does that look like in modern "post-leper" lives?

We embrace the forgiveness God has given to us with one hand, and with the other hand we extend grace and forgiveness to those who are needing it from us...sometimes even to ourselves.

One of the saddest things I've seen is women who know they are forgiven by God, yet for whatever reason they don't forgive themselves. They don't accept God's gift of forgiveness and the freedom that comes with His amazing gift. They allow themselves to remain in the bondage of regret, even though Jesus has opened the door and provided a way out. Their own self-induced punishment or disappointment in themselves keeps them chained down, unable to walk forward in their healing. Maybe it was the abortion they had that they now regret. Maybe it was the affair that cost them more than they were willing to pay. Maybe it was the father who betrayed their trust. Maybe it was that relationship that took more than they were willing to give.

If you are one of these women, I wish I could cup your beautiful face in my hands and say, "Jesus forgives you and can heal you. Embrace His forgiveness, His love, and His desire to make you whole again. You are dearly loved! Accept this amazing gift and walk forward in faith!"

Let's be women who not only accept the forgiveness of sin that Jesus so lavishly gives to us, but let's also be women who are "one of ten" women, grateful for the forgiveness and living with gratitude.

To those that much has been given, much is required (Luke 12:48).

Maybe there are those in your life needing to be told they are forgiven too. I know from my own experience with my daughter, Addie, it feels good to be forgiven. Let's all move forward in faith, step by step embracing the forgiveness we have been granted, and giving grace and forgiveness to those who are needing it from us. What better way to thank God for the forgiveness He has given to us than to extend it to others. May we be women who run back to our Lord with gratitude in our hearts and praise on our lips for the amazing work Jesus has done on our behalf, "giving thanks always and for everything to God the Father in the name of our Lord Jesus Christ" (Eph. 5:20).

Never forget, you are forgiven. Embrace that truth; let it soak down deep into your heart, and let the truth change you from the inside out. Then pass it on. Being thankful for what God has done for you, do the same for others.

PRAYER

Heavenly Father, we are so grateful that You are a faithful, forgiving God. We know that You have not dealt with us according to our sins nor rewarded us according to our iniquities. For as high as the heavens are above the earth, so great is Your loving-kindness toward those who fear you. May we live our lives with ever-increasing gratitude that You may be honored in all we say and do. In Jesus' name. Amen.

HALI'S TESTIMONY

On a cold day in January 2014, I found out my husband and I were expecting our first child. I couldn't be more excited and immediately began taking pictures of my belly and planned for the arrival of our child in just nine short months. We started buying items and told our families pretty early on. We went to our first doctor's visit and heard the heartbeat. We were both so full of joy and love for this little one.

A few weeks later it was time for our fourteen-week appointment. I had decided to go alone since my husband was working. I couldn't wait to see our little baby in the ultrasound and text the pictures to our family. As I lay there on the table and the nurse began the procedure, I could tell something wasn't quite right. I remember saying, "Our baby is really tiny in there." She didn't respond. I tried again, "Is it normal to be that small? I was expecting the baby to be a little bigger?" Again, no response.

Finally she spoke saying, "Do you think you could change into this gown? I'm going to call your doctor and have her take a look." The doctor couldn't find a heartbeat and told me I had miscarried.

I lost it. My world had just been shattered, and there I was, all by myself, crying and asking God, "Why?" I called my husband. He came to the hospital and we sat and cried together. Then we prayed.

The months that followed were so hard. I was devastated. My devastation turned into anger and bitterness. I would see pregnant women, even family members, and become full of hatred, sadness, helplessness, frustration, and many other emotions.

I didn't want to see or talk to people. I wanted to cry alone in my room. I didn't know how to handle it. I began to withdraw from my husband, feeling I'd let him down. I withdrew from my family as well. They seemed perfectly happy and their lives were moving on while I felt my life had stopped. I withdrew from God as I felt He had left me. I was filled with unanswered questions like, "Why me? Why did God take my baby? What did I do?"

I wanted to try to get pregnant again. Although I wasn't mentally prepared to face another pregnancy, I wanted to be a mom so badly. Shortly into January we found out we were pregnant again. My due date was in September. My marriage was a little stronger after walking through such a dark valley, but we were not as close as before because I still could not forgive myself or God. I prayed over every detail of the pregnancy but was fixated on losing the baby and was worried all day long. At eight weeks I began experiencing some complications. I called my doctor's office and said to the nurse, "I'm losing my baby again, aren't I?"

I did lose my second baby but, due in large part to the prayers of our church, family, and friends, experienced total peace.

A few months later, an opportunity presented itself for me to go on a mission trip to Nicaragua. While I was there, a pastor spoke about David and his battle with God over his son's death. It was so moving. The pastor then provided opportunity for others to share what God was doing in our lives and how He was working on the act of forgiveness. I felt God calling me forward, but I didn't want to go. What if they didn't see my past two years as a big deal? I still hadn't forgiven myself or God. What would I say about that?

Finally, a Nicaraguan woman spoke about how sick her son was and how she needed to rely on God to take care of him. She said they had to forgive God and themselves, as it was no one's fault that their son was so ill. After she finished, I felt the Lord stirring inside me. This time the pastor looked right at me, motioned in my direction and said,

"Does anyone else have something to share?" I was so nervous but stood up and prayed God would use me to minister to others.

I told of my struggles to forgive God for taking my babies away. As I shared my honest and raw emotions, I could feel God healing my heart, right there and then. After I spoke, the pastor called for prayer and paired me up with a Nicaraguan woman. We could not speak each other's language, but God bridged the gap. My partner and I cried together, and she hugged me and prayed loudly to God for me. She rubbed my stomach and cried uncontrollably. It was a powerful moment that changed the course of my life. In that moment I forgave myself and God. My heart was healing.

While in Nicaragua, I had been working through a personal Bible study on pregnancy and loss. A local pastor stopped me and asked if I would fast and pray with him and his wife during the next several days. I began fasting during breakfast, reading my Bible study and praying. Over the next few days, God revealed Himself to me in many different ways. The pastor and his wife prayed over me, with specific prayers for me to forgive God and trust in His plans. They prayed over my body, asking for healing and for life to fill my womb. I could truly feel the Holy Spirit for the first time in my life. As the week continued I started seeing and believing God loved me and was preparing me for motherhood. He wanted my heart to be completely His. He wanted my life to reflect Him and wanted my testimony to be shared with others so they could see Him through me.

When I returned from Nicaragua, my husband told me he thought I was pregnant. I didn't believe him and I didn't want to check, but the next day I woke early and felt the urge to take a pregnancy test. It was positive. I took another test. Again, positive.

I sank to the bathroom floor, crying uncontrollably and thanking God for loving me so much and giving me this gift. Throughout the entire pregnancy I had to really take time to keep my heart right with God and trust that He was in control. In March of this year I gave birth to the most beautiful baby girl, Hadley Grace.

For me, it's always been about my plan, what I thought was best. I've heard God say to me so many times, *Child, it's not about you, it's about Me and My plan.* And this scripture has really helped me: "For my thoughts are not your thoughts, neither are your ways my ways, declares the LORD. For as the heavens are higher than the earth, so are my ways higher than your ways and my thoughts than your thoughts" (Isaiah 55:8–9).

God used my times of trial as a way to grow me as a woman of faith, a mom, and a wife. My trust in the Lord and His plans grow daily. I trust Him with everything I have. I have forgiven God and forgiven myself.

Monday

READ: Psalm 103
SOAP: Psalm 103:10-11

Scripture - Write out the **Scripture** passage for the day.

Observations - Write down 1 or 2 **observations** from the passage.

Monday

Applications - Write down 1 or 2 **applications** from the passage.

Pray - Write out a **prayer** over what you learned from today's passage.

-Visit our website today for the corresponding blog post!-

Tuesday

READ: 1 Corinthians 15:50-57
SOAP: 1 Corinthians 15:57

Scripture - Write out the **Scripture** passage for the day.

Observations - Write down 1 or 2 **observations** from the passage.

Tuesday

Applications - Write down 1 or 2 **applications** from the passage.

Pray - Write out a **prayer** over what you learned from today's passage.

Wednesday

READ: Luke 17:11-19
SOAP: Luke 17:15-16

Scripture - Write out the **Scripture** passage for the day.

Observations - Write down 1 or 2 **observations** from the passage.

Wednesday

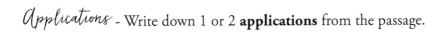

Applications - Write down 1 or 2 **applications** from the passage.

Pray - Write out a **prayer** over what you learned from today's passage.

-Visit our website today for the corresponding blog post!-

READ: Psalm 118:20-24
SOAP: Psalm 118:21

Scripture - Write out the **Scripture** passage for the day.

Observations - Write down 1 or 2 **observations** from the passage.

Thursday

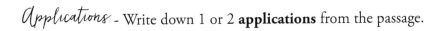

Applications - Write down 1 or 2 **applications** from the passage.

Pray - Write out a **prayer** over what you learned from today's passage.

Friday

READ: Ephesians 5:20
SOAP: Ephesians 5:20

Scripture - Write out the **Scripture** passage for the day.

Observations - Write down 1 or 2 **observations** from the passage.

Friday

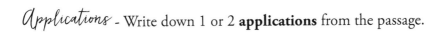

Applications - Write down 1 or 2 **applications** from the passage.

Pray - Write out a **prayer** over what you learned from today's passage.

-Visit our website today for the corresponding blog post!-

Reflection Questions

1. At what times are you tempted to doubt your calling and purpose? What do you do during these occasions to be transformed by the renewing of your mind?

2. Has there been those who have blessed you in some way but you've neglected to show your gratitude? Before the week passes, communicate your feelings to them, sharing how God used them to be a blessing to you.

3. List ten things about your relationship with Jesus you are grateful for, and thank Him for them.

4. Is there someone you need to ask for forgiveness? Pray that God would prepare your heart as you seek to live in peace with God and people.

5. Have you been holding anger against God? If so, confess your sin to Him and ask Him to enable you to learn to be content in every situation.

My Response

Week 7

Week 7 Challenge (Note: You can find this listed in our Monday blog post):

Prayer focus for this week: Spend time turning your fears into prayers.

	Praying	Praise
Monday		
Tuesday		
Wednesday		
Thursday		
Friday		

"I am overwhelmed with joy in the Lord my God! For he has dressed me with the clothing of salvation and draped me in a robe of righteousness. I am like a bridegroom dressed for his wedding or a bride with her jewels".

ISAIAH 61:10

Scripture for Week 7

MONDAY   *1 CORINTHIANS 13:4-13 (ESV)*

[4] Love is patient and kind; love does not envy or boast; it is not arrogant [5] or rude. It does not insist on its own way; it is not irritable or resentful; [6] it does not rejoice at wrongdoing, but rejoices with the truth. [7] Love bears all things, believes all things, hopes all things, endures all things.

[8] Love never ends. As for prophecies, they will pass away; as for tongues, they will cease; as for knowledge, it will pass away. [9] For we know in part and we prophesy in part, [10] but when the perfect comes, the partial will pass away. [11] When I was a child, I spoke like a child, I thought like a child, I reasoned like a child. When I became a man, I gave up childish ways. [12] For now we see in a mirror dimly, but then face to face. Now I know in part; then I shall know fully, even as I have been fully known.

[13] So now faith, hope, and love abide, these three; but the greatest of these is love.

TUESDAY   *1 JOHN 4:7-11 (ESV)*

[7] Beloved, let us love one another, for love is from God, and whoever loves has been born of God and knows God. [8] Anyone who does not love does not know God, because God is love. [9] In this the love of God was made manifest among us, that God sent his only Son into the world, so that we might live through him. [10] In this is love, not that we have loved God but that he loved us and sent his Son to be the propitiation for our sins. [11] Beloved, if God so loved us, we also ought to love one another.

WEDNESDAY   *JOHN 13:34-35 (ESV)*

[34] A new commandment I give to you, that you love one another: just as I have loved you, you also are to love one another.

^{35} By this all people will know that you are my disciples, if you have love for one another."

THURSDAY   *ISAIAH 61:10-11 (ESV)*

^{10} I will greatly rejoice in the Lord;

my soul shall exult in my God,

for he has clothed me with the garments of salvation;

he has covered me with the robe of righteousness,

as a bridegroom decks himself like a priest with a beautiful headdress,

and as a bride adorns herself with her jewels.

^{11} For as the earth brings forth its sprouts,

and as a garden causes what is sown in it to sprout up,

so the Lord God will cause righteousness and praise

to sprout up before all the nations.

FRIDAY   *HABAKKUK 3:17-19 (ESV)*

^{17} Though the fig tree should not blossom,

nor fruit be on the vines,

the produce of the olive fail

and the fields yield no food,

the flock be cut off from the fold

and there be no herd in the stalls,

^{18} yet I will rejoice in the Lord;

I will take joy in the God of my salvation.

^{19} God, the Lord, is my strength;

he makes my feet like the deer's;

he makes me tread on my high places.

To the choirmaster: with stringed instruments.

7

THE FRUIT OF OUR FORGIVENESS PART 2: LOVE AND JOY

BY WHITNEY DAUGHERTY

"The happiest people in the world are those who not only know they need to be deeply forgiven but also have experienced it."

-Tim Keller

On the Other Side of Redemption

MY WEARY ARMS overflowed with a humongous pile of filthy laundry, an all-too-fresh reminder of the stomach flu that had just invaded our household. I had just pulled an all-nighter with two very sick, needy little ones, and with barely enough energy to put together a coherent thought, I fell to my knees on my bedroom floor and asked God for more grace than I felt in that moment. As my prayer ended I lifted my head, took a deep breath, and tried to muster enough strength to head back into the battle that lay before me that day. But before I could even stand, my eyes unexpectedly met with a framed photo hanging on my bedroom wall, a picture of my husband and me on our wedding day.

I let out a nervous laugh so I wouldn't fall onto the floor in a heap of tears and exhaustion. Life had gotten messy and now looked very different from the future of bliss that I had pictured on my wedding day. The truth is, between work and school and responsibilities and sickness and all-nighters and *life*, I hadn't had one complete conversation with my husband in days. I missed him. I missed *us*.

Isn't it funny how one picture can take you back to every detail of life captured in that moment in time? The sights. The smells. The emotions. The season of life. It all flooded my memory at once, eliciting a depth of love and joy that had been muddied by the circumstances of life for far too long. Our wedding day had been a day of redemption. In my sale-rack wedding gown and Tyler in his sharp black tux, we knelt at the altar. But before we could gaze into each other's eyes and exchange carefree whispers and giggles, we prayed our guts out, hand in hand, until hot tears ran down our cheeks. It was a day when the old life surrendered to the new, when doubting, past relationships, loneliness, mistakes, heartache, and the waiting all fell under the umbrella of grace. It was a day when we committed *for life* a love that neither of us deserved. It was a day when we remembered who we were before Christ and how His extravagant love had transformed us and brought us to this place. The tears originated because of the depth of forgiveness we had received from God and each other, and they kept flowing because of the overwhelming love and joy that was now rooted down deep and available to us in abundance.

Unmeasurable love.

Unspeakable joy.

Made sweeter because we were now on the other side of redemption.

A baby's desperate cry came from upstairs and jolted me back into reality. I quickly glanced back up at the photo one last time before I was off to attend the heavy needs of the day. I studied our young, newlywed cheeks pressed together. My cheesy smile. Tyler's bloodshot eyes from his tears that ended up flowing throughout the ceremony. And in that moment, that depth of love and joy filled my heart once again. Circumstantially not much had changed: I still had sick babies, my body was still weary, and my laundry room was still filled to overflowing. But this time I rose to my feet with confidence, because on the other side of redemption, love and joy remain, even on the hardest of days.

Joy in the Bridegroom

> "I am overwhelmed with joy in the LORD my God! For he has dressed me with the clothing of salvation and draped me in a robe of righteousness. I am like a bridegroom dressed for his wedding or a bride with her jewels" (Isa. 61:10).

If you are in Christ—even if you are not yet or are never to be married in an earthly context —you are a betrothed bride. Your sin, under which you were once a slave, has been washed as white as snow by the Bridegroom Jesus, who has dressed you with the clothing of salvation and the robe of righteousness. Would you stop right now in whatever circumstance life finds you, look up, and ask Jesus to help you grasp the beauty of this imagery? The marriage of Christ and His church has been arranged by the Most High God, and the Bridegroom Jesus has chosen us, pursued us, with an everlasting love. So complete and supernatural and over the top is His love that He'll never get cold feet or leave us when the going gets tough. This love isn't conditional or respective of age, beauty, or season. This love remains in sickness and in health, in times of plenty and in times of want. So great is God's love for us that it holds firm on days when we *feel* like a bride, and even on the days when we wonder how in the world He could ever love someone as filthy and messed up as we are. Because the blood of Jesus has covered you, when God looks at you, He no longer sees your sin. Instead, you are like a bride dressed with jewels, adorned in His love, beauty, and grace: "For our sake he made him to be sin who knew no sin, so that in him we might become the righteousness of God" (2 Cor. 5:21). Have you forgotten that you don't have to perform to earn God's love for you? Nothing you can do will ever make God love you *more* than He loves you right now. Nothing you can do will ever make God love you *less* than He loves you right now. His love for you is unconditional, full, and complete. You are His child, beloved, and nothing can separate you from the love of Christ (Rom. 8:35–39). One day we will see the fullness of this love when the Bridegroom Jesus comes for His bride and takes us home to the place He has prepared for us. But as we wait for that day, we can live in great joy knowing that His love has conquered our sin, and in its place He has given us fullness of life through His resurrection power.

> "The LORD has done great things for us, and we are filled with joy" (Ps. 126:3 NIV).

Come to the Table

I'll never forget sitting leg to leg in those long wooden pews during our college days. We were not yet dating, but Tyler and I had developed a deep friendship that found us worshipping together in church most Sundays. After spending the first part of his college years searching and immersed in worldly living, Tyler's world was turned upside down by God. The man that sat next to me in church wasn't the same man I'd met years earlier in chemistry lab. The love of Jesus had transformed him. God's forgiveness was fresh and deep and real in his life. You could see it all over his face, and you could hear it in his passionate worship. Like the woman who lavished Jesus with expensive perfume, Tyler was a man who had been forgiven much, therefore he loved much (Luke 7:47). And witnessing him respond with uninhibited love and adoration for his Savior lit a fire in this girl who had become complacent in remembering the depth of which I had been forgiven. A. W. Pink wrote, "After grief for sin there should be joy for forgiveness."[1] When forgiveness is fresh in our hearts and minds we live life differently, don't we? Unfortunately, we are a distracted people who don't take time nearly as often as we should to remember what Jesus has done for us.

That's why Jesus commanded us to remember. He has asked us to come to the table, to take the bread and cup, and to recall His great love and forgiveness for wretched sinners like us (1 Cor. 11). And though that time of reflection begins as a somber event, it ends with great joy and celebration! This same God who spoke the world into existence— the One who turned the water into wine and made lepers clean—chose the cross so I could be raised from death to life. His sacrifice took on every last bit of my sin and shame. This is not just some story in a book that has recorded miracles from long ago. Oh, no. It is much, much more personal than that. This is *my* sin. This is *my* God. This is *my* story of redemption. And how can I not respond with overwhelming love and joy for all He has done for me? "Yet I will rejoice in the LORD; I will take joy in the God of my salvation. GOD, the Lord, is my strength; he makes my feet like the deer's; he makes me tread on my high places" (Hab. 3:18–19). Those God saves He sets on high places, where His safety and refuge protect and give new life. His forgiveness has rescued us and has rendered us "not guilty," granting us freedom and a spring in our step that wasn't there

---

1 A. W. Pink. *"A. W. Pink's Studies of the Scriptures 1934-1935."* 2005. Sovereign Grace Publishers.

before. If the love of Jesus has transformed us, God's forgiveness should be fresh and deep and real in our lives. The world should be able to see it all over our faces, and they should hear it in our passionate worship. Love and joy should spill over into all that we do, not some facade that we have manufactured out of obligation, but rather because this is our heart's overflow. This is our worship response to Jesus and His grace.

The most important question of this entire book is this: Do you know this Jesus and His turn-your-world-upside- down forgiveness?

And if you do, are you living like it?

Not of This World

> "We have this treasure in jars of clay, to show that the surpassing power belongs to God and not to us. We are afflicted in every way, but not crushed; perplexed, but not driven to despair; persecuted, but not forsaken; struck down, but not destroyed; always carrying in the body the death of Jesus, so that the life of Jesus may also be manifested in our bodies" (2 Cor. 4:7–10).

They stop us in our tracks because they live such a countercultural life. In a society that fights for what's right, fair, and easy, there is something radically different about these people. When you run across them, you can't miss them. And after you've been in their presence, you can't stop thinking about how stunning their behavior is. What they do simply doesn't make sense to the rest of the world, and they illicit the blaring question, What is it about these people that makes them so different? Maybe, like me, you've run across Jesus-followers in these places:

In the workplace: They're humble, and some of the hardest workers around. Instead of looking to advance their own personal agendas, they head to their jobs every day with the goal of serving others. When stressful work situations arise, they do their best to remain calm, bring peace, and rise above the negativity in the room. You might even see them praying in the break room before lunch or encouraging another employee who has been going through personal trials. They look for the best in others, are quick to admit when they're wrong, and are the first ones to give grace when others make mistakes.

At the local park: She's the mom with busy toddlers in tow, and from the smile on her face you'd never know she's only had four hours of sleep the night before. She's tired but her heart is full, and the love for her children is evident in each push of the swing, each low-to-the-ground hug, and in each sweet reminder as she follows right behind her little ones. She knows that these years can be messy, but she finds joy in small victories and embraces imperfection—both in herself and in her children—as opportunities to grow in patience and gentle training. Because of this, great joy overflows into the lives of her children.

> "Love is patient and kind; love does not envy or boast; it is not arrogant or rude. It does not insist on its own way; it is not irritable or resentful" (1 Cor. 13:4–5).

Across the street: You have a lot of nice neighbors, but there's just something about this crew that makes them stand out more than all the rest. They work together and they play together, but more than that, there's an overriding joy and peace that follows their family wherever they go. They invest in time and in teachable moments with their kids. They look for opportunities to love the neighbors around them (you've seen them shoveling that elderly couple's driveway more than once). And when that baseball came without warning from the yard next door and busted a hole in their fence? Grace, grace, and more grace.

> "A new commandment I give to you, that you love one another: just as I have loved you, you also are to love one another" (John 13:34).

Sitting in a hospital room: The diagnosis came, and it wasn't what they had hoped for. But they aren't shaken. They aren't bitter. They aren't hopeless. Instead, they look at this infirmity as an opportunity to shine the love of Jesus. They speak often of their faith to doctors, nurses, friends, and anyone who will listen. They tell of the strength and great purpose that God has brought to their lives through this trial. Instead of sadness, strangers are shocked to walk by and find laughter, singing, and praying coming from their room. People visit hoping to bring encouragement, but instead leave more encouraged than when they came. Life is hard and the future is unknown, but they are determined to love well and often, making every moment count.

Standing in the funeral receiving line: The joy that he has in sorrow really makes no sense to the rest of the world. After all, he's just experienced tremendous loss that many have labeled as "too soon" and "unfair." Some have questioned why things like this happen, but not him. His heart is peaceful, and his faith is sure. He knows that for those who love God, all things work together for good. He grieves, but he does not grieve without hope. In fact, in confronting death, Jesus has become even sweeter to him. With hands lifted high, he is moved to worship the One who has defeated death and offers eternal life for all who will place their faith in Him. Through the eyes of grace these Jesus-followers meet life head-on. They're forgiven, and so they're free.

Free to love.

Free to hope.

Free to dance.

Free to forgive.

Free to find joy.

Free to let go.

Free to truly live.

Returning to Your First Love

The pianist belted out the catchiest postlude rendition of "Joyful, Joyful, We Adore Thee" as we marched down the aisle as newly pronounced husband and wife. I'll never forget our wedding photographer saying that the shots taken immediately after the ceremony are always the most powerful because they capture the fresh elation of new life together. He even shared a story of one couple who reported to him years later that their wedding photographs had rekindled their marriage. In a time when their relationship was in turmoil, they looked back to photos from their wedding day and remembered how it all started. The love in their eyes. The vows before God. The commitment. The joy. The excitement and confidence of taking on the world united as one.

Evangelist Billy Graham said, "Jesus said . . . I'm the only way to permanent peace, I'm the only way to permanent joy, I'm the only way to eternal life, I'm the only way to forgiveness of sin, I'm the only way to the

Father."[2] Once we know this truth and receive it by faith, we are forever changed. But maybe you're in a season where the circumstances of your life have clouded the love and joy in Christ that you once knew. Maybe it's time you look back and remember how it all began. It's time you returned to your first love.

The truth is, between work or school, responsibilities or relationships, trials, and all of the temptations of the world, our time with God is up against some serious competition. If we're not careful, even the way we view God is challenged by how the world distorts and views Him. Maybe you've taken your eyes off of Him—off the cross—and it's been awhile since you've experienced the love and joy of those early days when God's forgiveness was fresh and deep and real in your life.

Our love for God and for others doesn't have to be manufactured when we remember the cross. Inexpressible joy can't help but overflow from us and onto others when we live daily in awe and wonder that Jesus has offered His forgiveness to us. Would you stop and take in the sights, the sounds, the emotions, the sacrifice, and the depth of forgiveness that happened that day on Calvary's hill? It was a day of redemption, and because of God's amazing love, the fruit of forgiveness—love and joy—is in turn available to you and to me in abundance.

"We love because he first loved us" (1 John 4:19).

PRAYER

Heavenly Father, we rejoice in the God of our salvation. You have dressed us with the clothing of salvation and draped us in a robe of righteousness. You make known to us the path of life; You will fill us with joy in Your presence, with eternal pleasures at Your right hand. Satisfy us in the morning with Your unfailing love so we may sing for joy and be glad all our days. We love You. In Jesus' name we pray. Amen.

---

2 Billy Graham. *"Peace With God."* 1953, 1984. W. Publishing Group

MELISSA'S TESTIMONY

I grew up in a preacher's home and was taught to be in God's Word. Knowing and loving God prepared me for what was to come. I married my high school sweetheart right after graduation. Shortly after we married, my husband got involved with some people that led him to drugs. We have been in a twenty-four-year battle with his drug addiction. He has relapsed repeatedly and our family has experienced a multitude of physical, emotional, and legal consequences resulting from his addiction.

The amazing thing about this story is that while I have biblical reasons for divorce, I have never been able to initiate the legal process. Our twenty-year-old daughter and our seventeen-year-old son have always supported my passion for my marriage. I have been employed at my church for a number of years, and one would think, given the circumstances, that my pastor and church family might support my leaving the marriage. But they, too, have encouraged me to not give up. Each I time move toward divorce, God has told me no, and I tell Him I don't understand why He won't release me.

Time after time, I have witnessed amazing blessings come as a result of my obedience. I can't explain why God has kept me faithful to an unfaithful mate, but at every point when I can't take anymore, God brings my husband back and, for a season, we see the man God wants him to be. As I've lived a life of obedience, I've witnessed my spiritual walk deepen, and I've become emotionally healthy. Increasingly, I'm learning how to set healthy boundaries as God has sustained me these long, difficult years. I believe one of God's purposes for keeping me in this marriage has been to make me stronger than I could have ever been any other way.

Up to this point, I have identified with Hosea when God spoke to him saying, "Go show your love to your wife again, though she is loved by another and is an adulteress. Love her as the LORD loves the Israelites" (Hos. 3:1 NIV). I have learned about a depth of forgiveness that I had never known. And regardless of the critical state of my marriage, I have experienced the deep love and joy of the Lord.

This past summer, our daughter left to go back to college for her second year. My husband began another spiral downward, leading to his arrest and twenty-eight days in jail. Upon his release he returned home and we witnessed him clean and sober, something we hadn't seen in a long, long time. He came to a crossroads ten weeks into his sobriety, and even though he professes to know the Lord, he continues to live in complete rebellion. When called to choose between light and dark, he did not surrender to the Lord, and I've asked him to leave.

For the first time in my marriage, I feel as though God may be moving me in a different direction. The children are unwilling to condone their father's behavior and have now distanced themselves from him. Up to this point, they had consistently wanted us to work it out, but now they are encouraging me to walk away. The children have observed my strength throughout the course of the marriage, and they remain grounded in God's Word themselves. We have all been faithfully trusting God.

I feel I may be nearing the end of my marriage. I have been obedient to God in the past and will follow His lead for my future. I believe God has used me over the years to encourage others to not be hasty to give up on their marriage, but if He is now leading me down a different path, I want to be obedient. It has always been the desire of my heart for my husband to be made whole, for my marriage to be restored, and my family to be intact.

In the process, God has taught me to love like He loves, to wait upon Him, even when I don't understand what He is doing, and to trust Him in all circumstances. I have been through the fire and learned the meaning of forgiveness, as God's power has been displayed through my circumstances. As I have waited upon Him in the past, I continue to wait upon Him now. I have made many mistakes throughout the years, yet God is maturing me through this journey. I know I could be angry and bitter, but God has given me the fruit of forgiveness, and I continue to live in His love and His joy despite all.

Monday

READ: 1 Corinthians 13:4-13
SOAP: 1 Corinthians 13:4-5

Scripture - Write out the **Scripture** passage for the day.

Observations - Write down 1 or 2 **observations** from the passage.

Monday

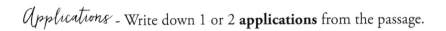

Applications - Write down 1 or 2 **applications** from the passage.

Pray - Write out a **prayer** over what you learned from today's passage.

-Visit our website today for the corresponding blog post!-

Tuesday

READ: 1 John 4:7-11
SOAP: 1 John 4:7

Scripture - Write out the **Scripture** passage for the day.

Observations - Write down 1 or 2 **observations** from the passage.

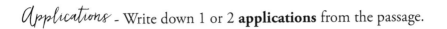

Applications - Write down 1 or 2 **applications** from the passage.

Pray - Write out a **prayer** over what you learned from today's passage.

Wednesday

READ: John 13:34-35
SOAP: John 13:34

Scripture - Write out the **Scripture** passage for the day.

Observations - Write down 1 or 2 **observations** from the passage.

Wednesday

Applications - Write down 1 or 2 **applications** from the passage.

Pray - Write out a **prayer** over what you learned from today's passage.

-Visit our website today for the corresponding blog post!-

READ: Isaiah 61:10-11
SOAP: Isaiah 61:10

Scripture - Write out the **Scripture** passage for the day.

Observations - Write down 1 or 2 **observations** from the passage.

Thursday

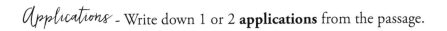

Applications - Write down 1 or 2 **applications** from the passage.

Pray - Write out a **prayer** over what you learned from today's passage.

Friday

READ: Habakkuk 3:17-19
SOAP: Habakkuk 3:18-19

Scripture - Write out the **Scripture** passage for the day.

Observations - Write down 1 or 2 **observations** from the passage.

Friday

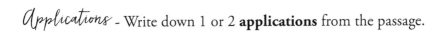

Applications - Write down 1 or 2 **applications** from the passage.

Pray - Write out a **prayer** over what you learned from today's passage.

-Visit our website today for the corresponding blog post!-

Reflection Questions

1. How does your life reflect the love and joy of your salvation?

2. Take time to reflect and journal how your love for Jesus and the forgiveness you have received from Him have influenced someone else.

3. How have you been blessed by striving to live a life of holiness and purity?

4. In what ways is the life of Jesus manifested in your body?

5. Spend time in God's Word and prayerfully ask Him to give you a renewed sense of awe at the wonder of your forgiveness and life in Christ.

My Response

Week 8

Week 8 Challenge (Note: You can find this listed in our Monday blog post):

Prayer focus for this week: Spend time thanking God for how he is working in your life.

	Praying	Praise
Monday		
Tuesday		
Wednesday		
Thursday		
Friday		

YOU ARE FORGIVEN

"How beautiful upon the mountains are the feet of him who brings good news, who publishes peace, who brings good news of happiness, who publishes salvation, who says to Zion, 'Your God reigns'".

ISAIAH 52:7

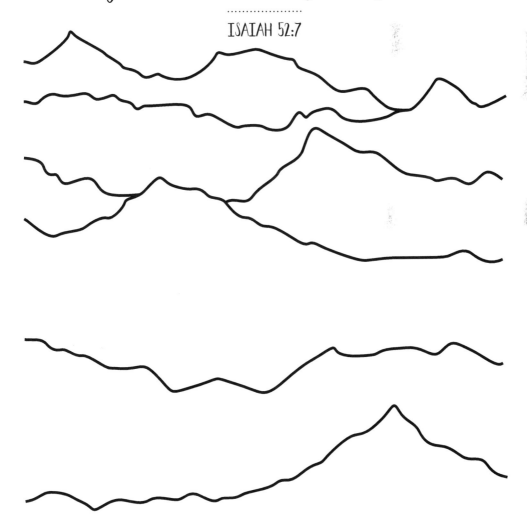

Scripture for Week 8

MONDAY   *2 CORINTHIANS 5:18-19 (ESV)*

[18] All this is from God, who through Christ reconciled us to himself and gave us the ministry of reconciliation; [19] that is, in Christ God was reconciling the world to himself, not counting their trespasses against them, and entrusting to us the message of reconciliation.

TUESDAY   *MATTHEW 28:16-20 (ESV)*

[16] Now the eleven disciples went to Galilee, to the mountain to which Jesus had directed them. [17] And when they saw him they worshiped him, but some doubted. [18] And Jesus came and said to them, "All authority in heaven and on earth has been given to me. [19] Go therefore and make disciples of all nations, baptizing them in the name of the Father and of the Son and of the Holy Spirit, [20] teaching them to observe all that I have commanded you. And behold, I am with you always, to the end of the age."

WEDNESDAY   *ISAIAH 52:6-8 (ESV)*

[6] Therefore my people shall know my name. Therefore in that day they shall know that it is I who speak; here I am."

[7] How beautiful upon the mountains
   are the feet of him who brings good news,
who publishes peace, who brings good news of happiness,
   who publishes salvation,
   who says to Zion, "Your God reigns."
[8] The voice of your watchmen—they lift up their voice;
   together they sing for joy;
for eye to eye they see
   the return of the Lord to Zion.

THURSDAY   *ROMANS 10:10-15 (ESV)*

¹⁰ For with the heart one believes and is justified, and with the mouth one confesses and is saved. ¹¹ For the Scripture says, "Everyone who believes in him will not be put to shame."¹² For there is no distinction between Jew and Greek; for the same Lord is Lord of all,bestowing his riches on all who call on him. ¹³ For "everyone who calls on the name of the Lord will be saved."

¹⁴ How then will they call on him in whom they have not believed? And how are they to believe in him of whom they have never heard? And how are they to hear without someone preaching? ¹⁵ And how are they to preach unless they are sent? As it is written, "How beautiful are the feet of those who preach the good news!"

FRIDAY   *MATTHEW 9:35-38 (ESV)*

³⁵ And Jesus went throughout all the cities and villages, teaching in their synagogues and proclaiming the gospel of the kingdom and healing every disease and every affliction. ³⁶ When he saw the crowds, he had compassion for them, because they were harassed and helpless,like sheep without a shepherd. ³⁷ Then he said to his disciples, "The harvest is plentiful, but the laborers are few; ³⁸ therefore pray earnestly to the Lord of the harvest to send out laborers into his harvest."

8

THE MESSAGE OF FORGIVENESS

BY ANGELA PERRITT

YOU ARE FORGIVEN. What powerful and life-changing words to hear when they are spoken to you.

I remember hearing a story once of a young man who sat in the front row of a church in Dallas, Texas. This young man was always eager to come to church, eager to worship Jesus, and eager to learn more about Him.

He wasn't like other men his age. He was different; he was joyful, and no one could deny his love for God.

After watching him for a few Sundays, passionately worshipping God during their worship time each week, one woman's curiosity got the best of her, and she wanted to meet this young man and find out more about him. So she did just that. One Sunday after the service, she approached him to find out his story and the reason for his joy. What she heard was a remarkable story on the power of forgiveness.

This young man had had a hard beginning to his life. He lived in one of the worst neighborhoods of his city and saw things his young eyes should never have seen. Bad influencers were everywhere, and over time he became like his environment. He became hardened. Things happened to him, and he began to view himself as "damaged goods."

A young man whose heart was once tender became cold and calloused. After years of seeing and experiencing violence, he himself became violent. The one who had once been the victim now changed roles and became the victimizer.

Then the worst night of his life happened. Through a series of terrible choices and an act of rage in a drug deal gone bad, he killed another young man his age. He tried to run and not get caught. He tried to avoid the punishment of his actions. But in the end, he was caught, found guilty, and sent to juvenile detention until his eighteenth birthday, when he'd be sent to prison.

In juvenile detention he tried to clean up his act, but the weight of what he had done always hung around his neck. When most young men were eager to get older he wasn't, because he knew prison was waiting for him on his eighteenth birthday. Then the day he had dreaded for years finally arrived; he was turning eighteen and was summoned to appear in court.

The judge sat solemnly behind his desk and addressed the young man as he entered the room, "Son, as you know, you have only served a few years out of your sentence for the death of the young man whose life you took. We have recently been contacted by the grandmother of that young man, the only living relative he had, and she has a few words she'd like to say to you." With that, an elderly woman came into the room and quietly stood before him.

With tears in her eyes, she looked into his and spoke these powerful words: "I forgive you. I forgive you for what you have done to me. I forgive you for taking the life of my dearly loved grandson, a boy I raised, loved, and cherished. I forgive you for the pain I have suffered and the loss of my dreams of watching him grow up and have a family of his own. I forgive you because Jesus has forgiven me for all the pain and heartbreak I have caused Him."

To this young man's astonishment, she then turned to the judge and asked him to waive the sentence for her grandson's death. In her words, "No sense in another boy losing his life." She wanted this young man to have another chance at life, and she knew the only way he could do that was through forgiveness.

And so in that small courtroom in Dallas, Texas, this young man was given just that, forgiveness and a second chance. It was something he couldn't earn and didn't deserve. And a young man's life was set free that day; the doors opened from his prison cell and a new life was birthed.

This young man is forever marked by the forgiveness he received, and his life is forever changed by it. So now every Sunday he comes to church excited and ready to worship his Lord, the Creator and giver of forgiveness, because he knows the cost of his freedom. His joy and gratitude characterize his life. It's true what they say, you know, those who have been forgiven much are the most joyful, because they know the price of their freedom.

We learned in the first chapter that through the choices of Adam and Eve and their original sin, we are all born into this world with a sinful nature. We are all guilty, and we all deserve death. Not one of us can ever be good enough to earn our salvation.

But oh how we are thankful for Jesus! Like the forgiven young man in the previous story, the forgiveness we have received due to Jesus' sacrifice should mark our lives too! His forgiveness sets us apart, and we are forever changed because of it.

God's forgiveness should saturate every part of our lives, and we should never be the same again because of it. As Scripture teaches, "Now all these things are from God, who reconciled us to Himself through Christ and gave us the ministry of reconciliation, namely, that God was in Christ reconciling the world to Himself, not counting their trespasses against them, and He has committed to us the word of reconciliation" (2 Cor. 5:18–19 NASB).

Because through Jesus' death we have received the forgiveness and payment for our sins, we now have a responsibility to help others experience this same reconciliation with God! Once we have experienced His grace, His love, and His forgiveness, we should want others in our lives to experience the freedom that His forgiveness gives.

It changes us from the inside out. Like the young man in my earlier story, this freedom, this forgiveness, permeates to all areas of our life! Life becomes sweeter, moments with loved ones more tender, hard times in life more endurable, and forgiveness more easily given.

What we have been given, we now want to give to others and so our ministry of reconciliation begins and never ends until the glorious moment we see Jesus face to face. So, with a heart full of God's love and a desire to see people set free through Jesus' redemptive forgiveness, we go out into our communities, we cross our neighborhood streets, and we reach across our dining room tables to share with those in our lives the good news of Jesus Christ.

We tell them about a God who loves them so much He actually died for their sins so they can be with Him in eternity. A God who is involved in our lives and sees it all. A God who is willing to forgive our most grievous sins and loves us in spite of them. A God who doesn't make us earn our salvation but rather offers it as a gift. A God who is for us, not against us. A God who loves us. A God who pursues us. And a God who says to go and share this good news with the world. "Go therefore and make disciples of all nations, baptizing them in the name of the Father and of the Son and the Holy Spirit, teaching them to observe all that I have commanded you. And behold, I am with you always, to the end of the age" (Matt. 28:19–20).

There are no geographical or cultural limits to this amazing ministry God has given to us. We are called to "go into all the world" (Mark 16:15), and so we do. Love God Greatly takes this command seriously. For our recent Bible study, our 150-plus page study journals were translated into more than eighteen languages and are available to download from our site. We are passionate about making sure Christians around the world have access to God's Word and have quality Bible study materials at their fingertips. Because of the amazing work God is doing through our translators, women in eighty-plus nations are digging into God's Word, learning to read and apply His Word to their lives.

Through the sacrifice of a few, many women are being blessed. Because a handful of women have taken Matthew 28:19–20 seriously and joined the ministry of reconciliation God has given to us, women's lives from around the world have forever been changed. Make no mistake; heaven has been changed because of these ordinary women in their homes, in their countries which have a passion for God's Word and a love for their women.

Actually, this very book that you have in your hands has been translated and sent out to the nations. For the first time many women are reading about God's amazing forgiveness and what that means for them personally. Through Scripture, they are finally able to understand God's grace, God's forgiveness, and are beginning to embrace the gracious gifts that have been offered to them through the Bible.

And one woman's life is changed because of God's forgiveness.

One woman's marriage is saved because she can now extend forgiveness to her husband because of the forgiveness she has received from God.

One prodigal son returns home because he is finally able to forgive himself for his past mistakes after he learns that Christ already has.

Life after life is changed because of the truth of this amazing forgiveness that is available only through Jesus Christ.

So how about you, sweet friend? Now that you've learned all about what sin is, how it came to be, and what has been done about it, can you take this head knowledge and actually turn it into heart knowledge?

I don't know your life. I don't know what you've been through, and I sure enough don't know the secrets you hold close to your heart, but God does. He knows it all. He sees it all, and yet He still chooses to love you and forgive you in spite of it. He pursues you with His relentless love, time and time again.

You may not feel like you deserve it, but no worries, none of us does. You're in good company.

As a friend, I want to take the time to ask you to accept God's gift of forgiveness. I see how holding on to past hurts, old grudges, and the replayed events in your mind are crippling you from the inside out. You may not think your unacceptance of God's forgiveness is having any effect on your life, but it is. It affects how you view yourself in the mirror. The type of relationships you allow yourself to have. It influences your expectations of others and makes your nights sleepless. Old wounds never heal and past mistakes are never redeemed because you refuse to let them go. Without even realizing it, you punish yourself.

Enough is enough.

If you can't do it for yourself, do it for those around you. Embrace God's forgiveness and then forgive yourself. You are the only one holding the keys to your prison cell. Through Christ's sacrifice and forgiveness, you have been granted freedom. But it's up to you. Will you choose to take the steps necessary to leave the prison of guilt, regret, and past mistakes? The door has been opened, but you must choose to walk out of it.

Take time this week to pray and ask God to help you embrace these gifts of forgiveness and grace we have been talking about. Never forget that our Lord was a friend to sinners. Though He is completely holy, He is also approachable. He is the loving Father many of us never had.

He is the prodigal's Father, who every day keeps His eyes on the horizon looking for the return of His son, His daughter. And He is the Father who runs to His children at the first sight of their coming home. Yes, God runs to you.

But, as Jesus said to His disciples, "The harvest is plentiful, but the laborers are few; therefore pray earnestly to the Lord of the harvest to send out laborers into his harvest" (Matt. 9:37–38).

Oh friend, this message of reconciliation and God's forgiveness needs to be taken out into the world! This grand story is unfolding through each life as we step out in faith and boldly take God at His Word.

A bountiful harvest is just waiting to be picked; there are women who need to hear your testimony of how God forgave you from your past sins and how your life changed as a result.

They need the hope that comes through accepting God's forgiveness and the changed life that comes from it. They need to know the Bible is not just another book filled with words and rules but indeed the very Word of God, and it's powerful enough to change lives, including theirs.

Friends, the harvest is plentiful. Go! "How beautiful upon the mountains are the feet of him who brings good news, who publishes peace, who brings good news of happiness, who publishes salvation, who says to Zion, 'Your God reigns'" (Isa. 52:7).

This is the message we send out into the world. We are forgiven and our lives are forever changed. And through Jesus, yours can be too!

But we ask, "How then will they call on him in whom they have not believed? And how are they to believe in him of whom they have never heard? And how are they to hear without someone preaching? And how are they to preach unless they are sent?" (Rom. 10:14–15)

You have a story to share. A message to give. And women are waiting who need to hear it. God is sending you out...go.

Reach out to those who are waiting:

- Your doctor

- Your neighbors

- Your children's teachers
- The lady at the store
- The single mom across the street

You are forgiven…now pass it on.

PRAYER

Heavenly Father, we are so grateful for the forgiveness that is ours through our Lord and Savior, Jesus Christ. We all have sinned and fall short of the glory of God. Yet You made a way for us to be forgiven from our sins. Reconciliation with You is possible through the blood of Jesus. Empower us, Holy Spirit, to lovingly share our joy with those who've not heard the good news of the Gospel of Jesus Christ. In His name we pray. Amen.

JOAN'S TESTIMONY

He said it was just tissue. In my heart I really didn't believe, it but if the doctor said it, it was true. When I went to have the abortion, the waiting room was full. Many of us sat on the floor waiting to be taken in for the procedure. I remember looking around me: this sea of young girls, eyes glazed over, everyone looking down, not making eye contact lest our shame and fear be observed. My girlfriend went with me for support. She knew where to go and what to do. She'd been there herself earlier in the month.

The procedure didn't take long, but the resulting grief was unending.

Years prior to that fateful day, the US Supreme Court decided in favor of Roe v. Wade and deemed that the US Constitution contained the right to have an abortion. My first child, along with a new estimated 57 million unborn babies, fell victim to that cultural holocaust. The decision to end my child's life within the first trimester, although sanctioned by the nation's legal system, could never be justified, excused, or reconciled by my own conscience. From that fateful day, a piece of me died with that baby, and I knew there was no way to undo the sorrow that now overshadowed my life.

Before I married, I made sure my husband knew about my past, and I shared openly with him about the abortion. His heart mourned for me as he observed the unrelenting grief over my unborn child. He attempted to comfort me with compassionate and tender words. Yet, as loving as he was, my regret remained unabated. The births of our two children only served to fortify in my mind the magnitude of my offense. This positioned me for a self-imposed exile from God. The inability to forgive myself kept me from seeking God, for I believed Him to be as despairing of me as I was of myself.

Spiritually bankrupt and without hope, I believed myself to be damaged beyond redemption and wore my shame and guilt as an ever-present cloak. I had walked away from my childhood religion and entered church as an adult only for weddings and funerals. God was not a driving force in my life, and though I did acknowledge Him, I did not pursue Him.

Saint Augustine wrote, "Thou hast made us for Thyself, O Lord, and our heart is restless until it finds its rest in Thee."[1] These words described my spiritual state during this time. I was tethered to the earth because of my love for my husband and children. Despite the unspeakable joy of loving and marrying my best friend and birthing two precious children, I remained unsettled, longing for something I couldn't express.

It was at this time a cousin invited me to join her at church. I heard the message of Jesus' death, burial, and resurrection. I understood that He died and took my sins upon Himself, and He saved me from eternal separation from God. I accepted Jesus' death as punishment for my past, present, and future sins. Then I surrendered my life to Jesus and prayed:

Dear Lord, I admit that I am a sinner. I have done many things that do not please You. I have lived my life for myself. I am sorry and I repent. I ask You to forgive me.

I believe that You died on the cross for me, to save me. You did what I could not do for myself. I come to You now and ask You to take control of my life. I give it to You. Help me to live every day in a way that pleases You.

1 Saint Augustine. *"The Confessions of St. Augustine."* AD 397; 1960. New York: Image Books.

I love You, Lord, and I thank You that I will spend all eternity with You. In Jesus' name. Amen."

One day while reading the Bible, I came upon this passage:

When Christ came as high priest of the good things that are now already here, he went through the greater and more perfect tabernacle that is not made with human hands, that is to say, is not a part of this creation. He did not enter by means of the blood of goats and calves; but he entered the Most Holy Place once for all by his own blood, thus obtaining eternal Redemption. The blood of goats and bulls and the ashes of a heifer sprinkled ceremonially unclean sanctify them so that they are outwardly clean. How much more, then, will the blood of Christ, who through the eternal Spirit offered himself unblemished to God, cleanse our consciences from acts that lead to death, so that we may serve the Living God! (Heb. 9:11–13 NIV)

After decades of living under a cloud of shame, guilt, sorrow, and tears, Jesus set me free. Through those words I came to understand that Jesus died to cleanse not only my sins but also my conscience from the remembrance of those sins. Why? So that I may serve the living God.

At once I realized that when my thoughts are continually focused inward, they cannot be focused upward. If God has forgiven me and Jesus paid for my forgiveness with His blood and His life, then how can I act as though what He did wasn't enough?

Through God's Word I was released and restored.

I will always regret my decision to deny life to my unborn child; that will never change. I have, however, forgiven myself to the degree that my guilt, shame, and pain are now under the blood of Jesus, and my freedom is used to bring honor and glory to Him.

With you there is forgiveness,
so that we can, with reverence, serve you.

(Ps. 130:4 NIV)

Monday

READ: 2 Corinthians 5:18-19
SOAP: 2 Corinthians 5:18-19

Scripture - Write out the **Scripture** passage for the day.

Observations - Write down 1 or 2 **observations** from the passage.

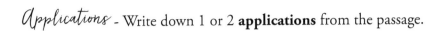

Applications - Write down 1 or 2 **applications** from the passage.

Pray - Write out a **prayer** over what you learned from today's passage.

-Visit our website today for the corresponding blog post!-

Tuesday

READ: Matthew 28:16-20
SOAP: Matthew 28:19-20

Scripture - Write out the **Scripture** passage for the day.

Observations - Write down 1 or 2 **observations** from the passage.

Tuesday

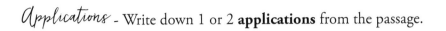

Applications - Write down 1 or 2 **applications** from the passage.

Pray - Write out a **prayer** over what you learned from today's passage.

Wednesday

READ: Isaiah 52:6-8

SOAP: Isaiah 52:7

Scripture - Write out the **Scripture** passage for the day.

Observations - Write down 1 or 2 **observations** from the passage.

YOU ARE FORGIVEN

Wednesday

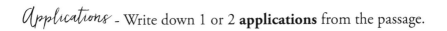

Applications - Write down 1 or 2 **applications** from the passage.

Pray - Write out a **prayer** over what you learned from today's passage.

-Visit our website today for the corresponding blog post!-

READ: Romans 10:10-15
SOAP: Romans 10:14-15

Scripture - Write out the **Scripture** passage for the day.

Observations - Write down 1 or 2 **observations** from the passage.

Thursday

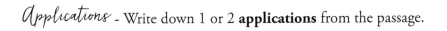

Applications - Write down 1 or 2 **applications** from the passage.

Pray - Write out a **prayer** over what you learned from today's passage.

Friday

READ: Matthew 9:35-38
SOAP: Matthew 9:37-38

Scripture - Write out the **Scripture** passage for the day.

Observations - Write down 1 or 2 **observations** from the passage.

Friday

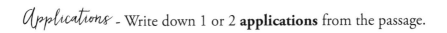

Applications - Write down 1 or 2 **applications** from the passage.

Pray - Write out a **prayer** over what you learned from today's passage.

-Visit our website today for the corresponding blog post!-

Reflection Questions

1. Have you ever felt like damaged goods? Confess those feelings to God, and then read Hebrews 9:11–13. Prayerfully ask God to allow you to relinquish your shame and guilt so you may serve Him, the Living God.

2. What actions do you continue to perform in order to be "good enough" to earn your salvation?

3. Prayerfully ask God to lead you to someone who needs to hear about the love of God. How might you tell that person about what Jesus has done for you?

4. What does God's grace and mercy mean to you?

5. You have been granted freedom in Christ! Choose today to walk out of your self-imposed prison, leaving your guilt and shame behind to serve the living God with a renewed heart!

My Response

How Can You Know That You Are Forgiven?

MANY NIGHTS WERE spent praying and writing this book (and then praying some more, begging Jesus for the words), and we believe that there's no better time to share from God's Word about what it really means to be forgiven.

We wanted a book that was real and raw – one that would let women know that they are not alone in the struggles of this life. The truth is, the team of women who contributed to this book sacrificed some serious guts and vulnerability in sharing their stories. Why would they do that? *Because Jesus is worthy*. Our prayer is that through these pages you'll be stunned by Jesus and His grace - either for the first time, or all over again - and that this truth will transform each of us so radically that it spills over into the hurting world around us.

But maybe you've read these pages and you still question whether God has really forgiven you.

We implore you - don't wait another day to embrace the love and forgiveness that Jesus has for you. How can you do that?

Know these truths from God's Word...

God loves you.

Even when you're feeling unworthy and like the world is stacked against you, God loves you - *yes, you* - and He has created you for great purpose.

> God's Word says, "God so loved the world that He gave His one and only Son, Jesus, that whoever believes in Him shall not perish, but have eternal life" (John 3:16).

Our sin separates us from God.

We are all sinners by nature and by choice, and because of this we are separated from God, who is holy.

> God's Word says, "All have sinned and fall short of the glory of God" (Romans 3:23).

Jesus died so that you might have life.

The consequence of sin is death, but your story doesn't have to end there! God's free gift of salvation is available to us because Jesus took the penalty for our sin when He died on the cross.

> God's Word says, "For the wages of sin is death, but the free gift of God is eternal life in Christ Jesus our Lord" (Romans 6:23); "God demonstrates His own love toward us, in that while we were yet sinners, Christ died for us" (Romans 5:8).

Jesus lives!

Death could not hold Him, and three days after His body was placed in the tomb Jesus rose again, defeating sin and death forever! He lives today in heaven and is preparing a place in eternity for all who believe in Him.

> God's Word says, "In my Father's house are many rooms. If it were not so, would I have told you that I go to prepare a place for you? And if I go and prepare a place for you, I will come again and will take you to myself, that where I am you may be also" (John 14:2-3).

Yes, you can KNOW that you are forgiven.

Accept Jesus as the only way to salvation...

Accepting Jesus as your Savior is not about what you can do, but rather about having faith in what Jesus has already done. It takes recognizing that you are a sinner, believing that Jesus died for your sins, and asking for forgiveness by placing your full trust in Jesus's work on the cross on your behalf.

God's Word says, "If you confess with your mouth that Jesus is Lord and believe in your heart that God raised him from the dead, you will be saved. For with the heart one believes and is justified, and with the mouth one confesses and is saved" (Romans 10:9-10).

Practically, what does that look like? With a sincere heart, you can pray a simple prayer like this:

God,

I know that I am a sinner.

I don't want to live another day without embracing the love and forgiveness that You have for me.

I ask for Your forgiveness.

I believe that You died for my sins and rose from the dead.

I surrender all that I am and ask You to be Lord of my life.

Help me to turn from my sin and follow You.

Teach me what it means to walk in freedom as I live under Your grace.

and help me to grow in Your ways as I seek to know You more.

Amen.

If you just prayed this prayer (or something similar in your own words), would you email us at info@lovegodgreatly.com? We'd love to help get you started on this exciting journey as a child of God!

About the Authors

ANGELA PERRITT is a writer, speaker, founder and director of LoveGodGreatly.com, a nonprofit online Bible study ministry that reaches thousands of women in over seventy countries with God's Word through their translated Bible studies. She and her husband live in Dallas, Texas with their three daughters. Angela's favorite titles in life are those of wife, mom, friend and daughter to the King of kings. She is passionate about God's Word and believes one woman in God's Word can change a family, community and ultimately a nation. Her greatest joy is to encourage her children and others to love God greatly with their lives....one day at a time.

JEN THORN spent most of her growing-up years in Germany. As a teen, she moved to Africa as a Missionary kid. She attended Moody Bible Institute in Chicago. It was at Moody that she met and married her best friend, Joe. Together they have 4 children: Katherine, Elias, Madeline, and Kilian. They live in the western suburbs of Chicago, where Joe is a pastor, and Jen homeschools their children.

Jen loves to cook and read. She hates getting up early, and longs for the day when all the rooms of her house are cleaned up at the same time! In this season of life God is teaching Jen self-sacrifice, discipline, the need for more organizational skills and how to apply the gospel to everyday situations and conversations. You can also find Jen on her personal blog, jenthorn.com.

JOY FORNEY is the proud wife of a missionary pilot and blessed mommy to five amazing kids. She and her family live in Uganda, Africa. She loves good books, great conversations, hot coffee, traveling the world, and most of all, Jesus. You can also find Joy at JoyForney.org where she blogs about missionary life, messy motherhood and the Gospel in the midst of the mundane.

WHITNEY DAUGHERTY has made a home with her husband Tyler since 1997, where there's never a dull moment raising three active boys and a hilarious little girl. A storyteller at heart, you can often find her writing and speaking to women about the lessons of everyday life, intertwining how God faithfully reveals Himself and gives much grace along the way. Whitney has a passion for God's Word, longs to love God and love people well, and prays that by God's grace, her children grow up to do the same.

Whitney serves as a writing contributor and editor for Love God Greatly, a global online Bible study community for women, and is Coordinator for the Global Advance Esther Initiative, whose mission is to empower women worldwide to become catalysts for God's purposes in their nations.

JOAN SHAFFER has been married to her God-given best friend, Bobby, for 37 years. They have been blessed with two precious children, their cherished spouses and five adorable and much-loved grandchildren. Thirty four years ago God mercifully became the Lord of Joan's life. From that moment she has been dedicated to serving Him faithfully. Whether advocating for children in the court system or leading women's Bible studies at her home church, she longs for others to know the love of Jesus that transformed her life. Romans 8:37-39.

a LoveGodGreatly Bible Study Journal

David

HIS STORY IS OUR STORY

Welcome, friend. We're so glad you're here...

LOVE GOD GREATLY exists to inspire, encourage, and equip women all over the world to make God's Word a priority in their lives.

-INSPIRE-

women to make God's Word a priority in their daily lives through our Bible study resources.

-ENCOURAGE-

women in their daily walks with God through online community and personal accountability.

-EQUIP-

women to grow in their faith, so that they can effectively reach others for Christ.

Love God Greatly consists of a beautiful community of women who use a variety of technology platforms to keep each other accountable in God's Word.

We start with a simple Bible reading plan, but it doesn't stop there.

Some gather in homes and churches locally, while others connect online with women across the globe. Whatever the method, we lovingly lock arms and unite for this purpose...

to Love God Greatly with our lives.

At *Love God Greatly*, you'll find real, authentic women. Women who are imperfect, yet forgiven. Women who desire less of us, and a whole lot more of Jesus. Women who long to know God through his Word, because we know that Truth transforms and sets us free. ***Women who are better together, saturated in God's Word and in community with one another.***

Love God Greatly is a 501 (C) (3) non-profit organization. Funding for Love God Greatly comes through donations and proceeds from our online Bible study journals and books. LGG is committed to providing quality Bible study materials and believes finances should never get in the way of a woman being able to participate in one of our studies. All LGG journals and translated journals are available to downloaded for free from LoveGodGreatly.com for those who cannot afford to purchase them. Our journals and books are also available for sale on Amazon. Search for "Love God Greatly" so see all our Bible study journals and books. 100% of proceeds go directly back into supporting Love God Greatly and helping us inspire, encourage and equip women all over the world with God's Word.

THANK YOU for partnering with us!

What we offer:

18 + Translations | Bible Reading Plans | Online Bible Study
Love God Greatly App | 80 + Countries Served
Bible Study Journals & Books | Community Groups

Each Love God Greatly study includes:

Three Devotional Coorsesponding Blog Posts | Monday Vlog Videos
Memory Verses | Weekly Challenge | Weekly Reading Plan
Reflection Questions And More!

Other Love God Greatly studies include:

David | Ecclesiastes | Growing Through Prayer | Names Of God
Galatians | Psalm 119 | 1St & 2Nd Peter | Made For Community | Esther
The Road To Christmas | The Source Of Gratitude | You Are Loved

YOU CAN FIND US ONLINE AT LOVEGODGREATLY.COM

54463930R00143

Made in the USA
Lexington, KY
17 August 2016